Read Me First

- Descriptions in this manual are based on what is available as at the time of writing this guide, and it may not be 100% accurate again if there is a major software update to All-New Fire HD 8 Tablet (6th Generation, 2016 Edition).

- All information supplied in this guide is for educational purpose only and users bear the responsibility for using it.

- Although I took tremendous effort to ensure that all information provided in this guide are correct, I will welcome your suggestions if you find out that any information provided in this guide is inadequate or you find a better way of doing some of the actions mentioned in this guide. All correspondence should be sent to pharmibrahimguides@gmail.com

About This Guide

This is a very thorough, no-nonsense guide, useful for both experts and newbies.

Also including:

- *Extensive guide on Alexa*
- *How to sideload apps (including Google Play store) on All-New Fire HD 8 Tablet.*

This is a very detailed and extensive guide on All-New Fire HD 8 Tablet (6th Generation, 2016 Edition). It is full of actionable steps, hints, notes, screenshots and suggestions. This guide is particularly useful for newbies and seniors; nevertheless I strongly believe that even the techy guys will find benefits reading it.

Enjoy yourself as you go through this very comprehensive guide.

PS: Please make sure you don't give the gift of All-New Fire HD 8 Tablet (6th Generation, 2016 Edition) without given this companion guide alongside with it. This guide makes your gift a complete one.

Table of Contents

Getting Started With Your Tablet 1

Unpacking Your Device.. 1

Turning your Tablet on and off.. 1

Get to know your device.. 3

Inserting and Managing SD Card 4

Using the touch screen 7

Navigating Apps on the Fire HD 8 tablet...................................... 10

The Back Button 10

Getting to know Your Home Screen 11

Accessing Applications 13

Customizing Your Tablet.. 15

Entering a text.. 20

Airplane mode 22

Using The New Features..23

Alexa.. 23

The Word Runner 24

The Amazon Underground 24

Using The Web and the Apps 26

Silk Browser 26

Using other Fire tablet apps 39

Communication..40

Using The Email App... 40

Using Facebook and Twitter...43

Personal Information 44

Contacts 44

Accessibility Features – The Special features for easy usage...........47

VoiceView Demystified..47
Using the VoiceView...49
Reading with VoiceView..52

Screen Magnifier 55

Using the Braille with Fire HD 8 Tablet 56

Managing The Hearing Settings..57

TOOLS 60

Amazon FreeTime Demystified...60

Understanding Amazon Household and Family Library 66

A Comprehensive Guide on Reading Books on Your Device 73
Reading a book..73
Syncing to furthest page read 76
X-Ray feature...76
Blue Shade...79
Sharing a text/passage 80
Bookmarking a Page 80
Managing highlights 81
Managing notes...82
Dictionary 84
Wikipedia...84
Using the Flashcards 85
Word Wise..86
Using the Word Runner 87
Using Text-to-Speech 89

Creating schedules and more with the Calendar...............................90

Managing your document with 'Docs' 93

Connectivity 95

PC Connections..95

Wi-Fi 97

Access More By Using Bluetooth 99

Location Services 100

Find My Device Feature 101

Entertainment **104**

Using the Camera 104

Recording a video 107

Using the Video Player 110

Media Player Virtual Keys 111

Settings **113**

Wireless 113

Storage 113

Power 115

Apps & Games 117

Display 118

Device Options 119

My Accounts 122

Profiles & Family Library 123

Parental Controls 123

Security 125

Sounds & Notifications 126

Keyboard & Language 126

Sync Device 127

Help 127

Accessibility 128

Legal & Compliance 128

What You Must Know About Your Fire Tablet **129**

Removing Special Offers Banner 129

How to take screenshot on your device...130

How To Find Your Tablet When lost 130

Amazon Limited App – You have little To Worry About 131

How to Access Google Drive And Other Cloud Drives Easily.............134

Solution to Non-Responding Apps..135

How To conserve Fire Tablet's Battery Life 136

How to read EPUB on your device..138

How to send personal document to your fire tablet or any Kindle device.......139

Extras **142**

Getting an antivirus for your tablet -- is it necessary? 142

Safety Precautions When Using Fire Tablet on Wi-Fi 143

I am Having a Dwindling Love for my Fire Tablet; What Should I do? 145

How to Sideload Google Play Store on Fire Tablet 146

Troubleshooting **148**

Safety precautions... **152**

Bonus Chapter.. **154**

Alexa...154
   Disabling/Enabling Alexa 154
   Speaking to Alexa 155
   Using Alexa to open Apps or Programs 156
   Using Alexa with Different Types of Skills 156
   Connecting Your Smart Devices to Alexa 158
   Grouping Your Smart Home Devices 160
   Using Alexa with Smart Home Devices..161
   Using Alexa with Your Calendar 162
   Using Alexa with Your Shopping List and To-do List....................164
   Using Alexa with Alarm 166
   Using Alexa with Timer...168
   Using Alexa with Clock 170
   Using Alexa to Get Flight Information 170

Listen to Your Audiobooks.. 171
Read Kindle Books with Alexa 173
Buying Items Using Your Voice 174
Using Alexa to Get Traffic Information 176
What about Math? 177
Using Alexa to get definitions.. 177
Using Alexa with Wikipedia 178
Using Alexa To Get General Information................................... 178
Funny sides of Alexa 178
Alexa's Settings 179
Troubleshooting Alexa.. 180

Just Before You Go (Please Read!).. *181*

How to Use This Guide

This guide is an unofficial manual of All-New Fire HD 8 Tablet (6th Generation, 2016 Edition) and it should be used just like you use any reference book or manual.

To quickly find a topic, please use the table of contents. This will allow you to quickly find information and save time.

Lastly, when you are asked to tap a switch next to an item, just tap the box containing the switch. The switch should become colored when it is **On.**

I hope this guide helps you get the most out of your Fire tablet.

Getting Started With Your Tablet

Unpacking Your Device

When you unpack your product box, check your product box for the following items:

1. All-New Fire HD 8 Tablet (6th Generation).

2. USB 2.0 charging cable & 5W power adapter

3. Quick Start Guide

Hint: To charge your tablet in a faster manner, get **9W Power adaptor** made by Amazon. This adaptor will charge your tablet in an accelerated manner. And guess what; the adaptor is compatible with All-New Fire HD 8 Tablet (6th Generation, 2016 Edition).

Turning your Tablet on and off

To turn on your tablet, press and hold the Power Key. If you turn on your tablet for the first time, follow the on-screen instructions to set it up.

To turn off your tablet, press and hold the power key and select **OK.**

To restart your device, press and hold the power button until the device restarts automatically. Please note that you may need to press and hold your device for up to 40 seconds before you get your device restarted.

Note: It is advisable to charge your tablet before you set it up. However, if your device is fully charged when you received it, you may not need to charge it before using it. When your device is charging, you will see this icon at the top right corner of the screen.

In addition, using another power adaptor (other than the one that came with it) to charge your device may increase charging time. If you need to use another charger to charge your tablet, then visit this webpage **http://pharmibrahim.blogspot.com/2015/10/blog-post.html** for a list recommended chargers.

Get to know your device

Device Layout

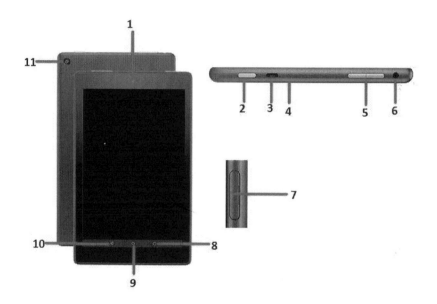

Number	Function
1.	Front facing camera
2.	Power Button
3.	Micro-B USB Port

4.	Microphone
5.	Volume button
6.	Headset Jack Port
7.	Micro SD Card Slot
8.	Task Switcher button
9.	Home Button
10.	Back Button
11.	Rear-Facing Camera

Inserting and Managing SD Card

Fire tablet supports the use of external memory card and you can add a microSD card for up to 200 GB.

To insert memory card:

1. Hold your tablet making sure the front camera is facing you and the power button is up.(see the picture below)
2. Gently open the SD card slot on your device.
3. Hold your memory card and make sure that cover is facing up as shown below.
4. Gently slide in the memory card and make sure it fits in.

To remove the SD card:

1. Swipe down from the top of the screen and select **Settings.**

2. Tap **Storage**

3. Tap **Safely Remove SD Card** and tap **OK.**

4. Gently open the SD Card slot and then gently press the SD Card to remove it. Close the SD Card slot when you are done.

Managing Your SD Card

You can manage how your device use your SD Card.

To turn off the SD Card surpport for a particular content category (such as books):

Please note that this feature is turned on for all surported categories by default.

1. Swipe down from the top of the screen and tap **Settings**, and then tap **Storage**.
2. Under SD Card, tap a switch next to a content category to turn MicroSD card support off.
3. To manage a particular content stored on SD Card, tap on **SD Card Storage** and then tap on the content you want to manage.

Notes:

1. Unless you disable the feature, all supported apps are automatically installed on your SD Card. In addition, downloaded video files and photos and videos taken with camera will also be saved on your SD Card unless you disable the feature.
2. If you have multiple profiles on your device, videos downloaded to the MicroSD Card will only be available to the profile that downloaded it. In addition, photos and personal videos stored on SD Card will only be available to profile that stored them. However, photos and personal videos that are transferred to your Fire tablet via USB or that were previously downloaded to a MicroSD card (before the creation of multiple profiles) will be available to all adult profiles.

To transfer apps from internal storage to SD Card:

1. Swipe down from the top of the screen and tap **Settings**, and then tap **Apps & Games**.
2. Tap **Manage All Applications.**
3. Select the app you want to transfer
4. Tap **Move to SD Card**

Downside: As at the time of writing this guide, it appears that the only way to move a downloaded video from internal storage to your MicroSD card is to delete it from your device, and then re-download it again.

Using the touch screen

Your tablet's touch screen allows you to easily select items or perform functions.

Notes:

- Do not press the touch screen with your fingertips, or use sharp tools on the touch screen. Doing so may damage the touch screen or cause it to malfunction.
- Do not allow the touch screen to come into contact with other electrical appliances. This may cause the touch screen to malfunction.

- Do not allow the touch screen to come in contact with water. YOUR DEVICE IS NOT WATER RESISTANT. The touch screen may malfunction in humid conditions or when exposed to water.
- For optimal use of the screen, you may need to remove screen protector before using it. However, a good screen protector should be fully compatible and usable with your device.

You may control your touch screen with the following actions:

Tap: Touch once with your finger to select or launch a menu, application or option.

Tap and hold: Tap an item and hold it for more than a second to open a list of options.

Tap and drag: Tap and drag with your finger to move an item to a different location in the application grid/list.

Pinch: Place two fingers far apart, and then draw them closer together.

> **To Lock or Unlock the touch screen**

When you do not use the device for a specified period, your device turns off the touch screen and automatically locks the touch screen so as to prevent any unwanted device operations and also save battery. To manually lock the touch screen, press the power key once.

To unlock, turn on the screen by pressing the power key and then swipe to unlock. If you have already set a lock screen password, you will be prompted to enter the password.

Note: You can activate the screen lock feature to prevent unwanted access to your tablet, to learn more please refer to page 18.

Rotating the touch screen

Your tablet has a built-in motion sensor that detects its orientation. If you rotate the device, the interface will automatically rotate according to the orientation. If you rotate your device horizontally, your device will change to Landscape mode, and if you rotate your device vertically, your device will enter Portrait mode.

➢ **Activating and deactivating screen rotation**

You may deactivate or activate screen rotation by following these steps:

1. To deactivate screen rotation, swipe down from the top of the screen to bring out **Quick actions menu.**
2. Tap on **Auto-Rotate** (So that it fades out and becomes grey)
3. To activate, tap on **Auto-Rotate** again (So that it becomes bold)

Navigating Apps on the Fire HD 8 tablet

You can navigate apps on your tablet using the left and right panels. The left and right panels give you more information about what you are viewing. To bring out the right panel, swipe from the right edge of the screen. To bring out the left panel, swipe from the left edge of the screen.

The main difference between the left and right panel is that the left panel gives you the menu information of an app while the right panel allows you to navigate the content page for items like books.

The Back Button

I am including the back button under the getting started chapter because you will be using this feature a lot. Whenever you are done with a setting or feature and you don't see the **Done** button, you should consider using the back button. It is a smart way to get out of a menu when you are stuck and don't know what next to tap. There are two buttons that can serve the purpose of back button on your device and they are:

1. **The small triangle button**: This is a small trangular button ◁ located at the bottom of the screen (beside the home button). Usually, tapping on this icon will take you back to the previous page.

2. **The small arrow button**: In some app pane, you will find another button that can serve as a back button. This button is a small arrow-like button usually locates at the upper left corner of the screen. Please note that not all app panes will display this button. In fact, you may find out many app pane does not contain anything like this.

Tip: You may use any of the back buttons described above to get out of any page when you are done with the page and you don't see the done option.

Getting to know Your Home Screen

From your home screen, you can search for items and access applications. Swipe your finger up or down to see different apps on the home screen. You can also perform quickly organize similar apps by tapping and dragging one app on top of the other. In addition, you can move an app from one location to another on the home screen by tapping and dragging it.

Home screen has two different portions:

1. **The search portion:** This displays a search bar on top of the app grid. You can use this search bar to quickly find an item.

2. **The app grid portion:** This displays all the available apps in grid format. New apps you download are automatically added to the app grid. Once added to the app grid, the app will remain there until you remove it by uninstalling it.

Removing items/apps from the home screen

1. When on the home, tap and hold an item to open a list of options.

2. Select **'Uninstall'**

Note: Selecting **Uninstall** will remove the app permanently from your device. In addition, Fire tablet comes preloaded with some apps and you may not able to remove these preinstalled apps.

Home Screen Categories

The home screen has many categories and you can switch between them by swiping left or right. The categories include Books, Video, Games, Shop etc. You can also switch between different categories by tapping on their name.

Category bar

When you are in a particular category page, you have access to two options namely:

Library: This gives you access to all of your items.

Store: This gives you access to Amazon webpage.

To Move an Item on the Application Grid Screen

1. Launch the application grid by pressing the home screen button.
2. Tap and hold an item to move.
3. Drag the item to the location you want.

To create a folder of items/apps

1. From the home screen, tap and hold an item, then drag and drop it directly on top of another item/app's icon to create a folder.

Accessing Applications

1. Press the Home screen button to access application grid.

2. Tap on the app of your choice

3. To go back to the app grid screen, press the back button ◁ or the home button ◯ (the buttons located at the bottom of the screen). If these buttons are not showing, tap the middle of the screen or swipe up from the bottom of the screen to bring them to view.

Accessing Recently Opened or Running Applications

1. Tap on the task-switcher button ▣ (the button beside the home button) to see all recently opened apps or items. This should contain all the opened/running apps.
2. Tap on the app to launch it, or tap on the **X** icon to close it.

Note: Although your tablet can run more than one app at the same time, multitasking may cause hangs-ups, freezing, memory problems, or additional power consumption. To avoid these, end all unused programs by closing the app.

Tip: You may consider installing app like **ES Task Manager** from the Amazon Appstore in order to better manage your apps.

Customizing Your Tablet

Changing the device language

The device language is integrated with the keyboard language and this means that if you change your device language, the onscreen keyboard will also change automatically and assume the device language. See the next section to learn how to manually change your keyboard language.

If you are turning your tablet on for the first time, you have the option to select a language of your choice. To change the language setting at any time, follow these steps:

1. Swipe down from the top of the screen to open the quick actions menu, and then tap **Settings**. Alternatively, you may open the application grid and tap on the settings icon.
2. Scroll down and tap on **Keyboard & Language.**
3. Tap on **Language**.
4. Select a language from the list.

To change the keyboard language

1. Swipe down from the top of the screen to open the quick actions menu, and then tap **Settings**. Alternatively, you may open the application grid and tap on the settings icon.
2. Scroll down and tap on **Keyboard & Language.**
3. Tap on **Current Keyboard** and make sure **Fire Keyboard** is selected.

4. Tap **Keyboard Settings.**

5. Tap on **Keyboard Language**

6. Then tap on the switch next to **Use system language** to select the language you want. To remove a language, tap the switch next to that Language.

7. To download a new language, tap **Download Languages,** and then select the new language you want to download. You may need to accept the Terms of service if you are downloading the keyboard language for the first time.

8. To delete a language, tap the language you want to delete and then select **Yes** to confirm.

Hint: To quickly change your keyboard language while using the keyboard, long press the virtual **Spacebar** on the keyboard and then select the language of your choice.

Set the current time and date

1. Swipe down from the top of the screen to open the quick actions menu, and then tap **Settings**.

2. Tap on **Device Options**.

3. Then tap on **Date & Time**. In addition, you may also turn **On/Off** the Automatic Time Zone. If this option is turn On, your device will try to determine your time zone and update to the date and time for that zone when you are connected to the internet.

To manage notification and sounds options

1. Swipe down from the top of the screen to open the quick actions menu, and then tap **Settings**.
2. Tap on **Sounds & Notifications**
3. Tap on **Default Notification Sound** and select your preferred sound.
4. To manage how you see your notifications while your device is locked, tap of **When Device is Locked.**
5. To select which app can send you notifications, tap on **App Notifications** to choose your preferred apps.

Hint: To completely mute your device if you don't want any distraction, swipe down from the top of the screen and tap **Do Not Disturb.**

To adjust the tablet's volume or switch to silent mode

1. Press the Volume key up or down, this brings up the volume panel.
2. Use the volume keys to adjust the volume of your tablet as you like.
3. To mute all sound, swipe down from the top of the screen to open quick actions menu and tap on **Do Not Disturb.**

Adjusting the brightness of the display

1. Swipe down from the top of the screen to open the quick actions menu
2. Drag the slider to adjust the brightness.

Hint: The brightness level of the display will affect how quickly the device consumes battery power. I will advise that you turn it reasonably low if you are very concerned about saving your battery.

To set screen lock password or PIN or change the automatic lock time

You can lock your tablet by activating the screen lock feature. *Note:* Once you set a screen lock, your tablet will require an unlock code each time you turn it on or unlock the touch screen.

1. Swipe down from the top of the screen to open the quick actions menu, and then tap **Settings**. Alternatively, you may open the application grid and tap on the settings icon. Then scroll down and tap on **Security**.
2. Tap the switch next to **Lock Screen Passcode.**
3. Tap **PIN** or **Password** and enter the **PIN/ Password** you like.
4. To change your pin/password, tap **Change Passcode.**

Notes:

1. Setting a passcode is a nice way to prevent unwanted access to your device. I will recommend that you use a password to lock your device instead of using a pin. A password combine letters, numbers, and special characters and therefore provide more security than pin.

2. If you plan to setup Amazon FreeTime profiles on your device, please note that the lock screen password/pin must be turn on. It is part of requirement for setting up FreeTime profiles. To learn more about Amazon FreeTime, please go to page 60.

Hint: Swipe down from the top of the screen to view your recent notifications while the screen is locked. But you will need to unlock your device by entering your pin/password (if you have any) to view your notifications details.

Setting a wallpaper

1. Swipe down from the top of the screen to open the quick actions menu, and then tap **Settings**.
2. Tap on **Display**.
3. Tap on **Wallpaper** and follow the onscreen instructions to complete the process.

Entering a text

You can enter text by selecting characters on the virtual keypad.

Note: You can change the writing language to any one supported. For more information refer to page 15.

To enter text:

1. Enter text by selecting the corresponding alphabet or numbers.

2. You can use any of the following keys:

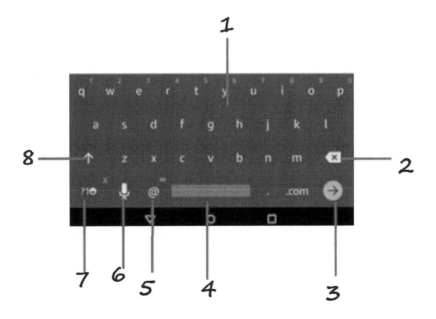

Number	Function
1.	Virtual keyboard alphabets

2.	Clear your input/backspace
3.	Start a new line or launch a webpage
4.	Spacebar. To quickly change your keyboard language while using the keyboard, long press this spacebar key and then select the language of your choice.
5.	Tap and hold on the key to split your keyboard into two.
6.	Use the voice command feature
7.	Switch between Number, Symbol and Emoticon mode. If you look closely at the ?1☺ key, you will see that there is a small scissor icon on the key. **See below** (the next page) to learn more on how to use this functionality. **Hint:** To return to ABC mode, tap on the **ABC** key located on the keyboard.
8.	Change case

Tips:

1. When entering a web address, press and hold on the **.com** key to get access to other variants like .gov, .co.uk etc.

To copy and paste a text

While you are entering text, you can use the copy and paste feature.

1. Tap and hold a word, and then drag to select the text you want

2. Then select "Copy button" to copy, or select "Cut button" to cut the text onto the clipboard

3. In another application or where you want to place the text, tap and hold the text input field.

4. Then select "Paste button" to insert the text from the clipboard into the text input field.

5. To use the onscreen keyboard copy and paste buttons, tap and hold on **ABC** or **?1☺.**

Airplane mode

In airplane mode, you can disable all wireless connections and network connection. This may be important in hospitals and airports. This feature also helps you save battery power.

1. Swipe down from the top of the screen to open the quick actions panel.

2. Tap on the **Airplane Mode** button.

Using The New Features

All-New Fire HD 8 Tablet (6th Generation) came with special features that differentiate them from other Fire tablets. The main two new features that came with the new Fire tablets are discussed below.

Alexa

Amazon has finally decided to include its virtual assistant on Fire tablets. Alexa will transform the way you use your Fire tablet. I have written a very extensive guide on Alexa, please refer to page 154 of this guide to learn more.

The Word Runner

This feature allows you to fix your gaze on the tablet while the words you are reading move by themselves. It saves you the effort of moving your look to different parts of the screen in order to read a book. This feature is also made in such a way that it automatically slows down when comes across a difficult word or punctuation.

You have the option to choose a speed with which this feature move words when you are reading a book. If you miss something while reading, tap and hold the screen to pause the Word Runner. When you are done, just release the screen. To learn more about word runner, please go to page 24.

The Amazon Underground

Amazon Underground is another new feature on All-New Fire HD 8 Tablet (6th Generation). It features all of the functionality of the regular Amazon mobile shopping app and in addition gives you access to a large number of paid apps for free.

With this new feature, instead of you paying for an app, Amazon will pay the app developer based on the amount of time you spent using the app. In a way, I think Amazon is trying to woo app developers to develop more engaging apps for its Appstore.

According to Amazon, over $20,000 apps/apps related items are free with Amazon Underground.

Purchase of Fire tablet gives you automatic access to Amazon Underground.

Using The Web and the Apps

Silk Browser

Fire tablet is preloaded with Silk browser to cater for your browsing needs. Please note that the information provided here may vary if Amazon makes any update to silk browser.

> ➢ **To browse web pages**

1. Open the silk browser by tapping **silk browser icon** on the home screen.

2. Type the web address into the URL input field, and tap search/go button (the arrow button on the virtual keyboard). As you type into the address bar, Silk browser will make search suggestions based on your default search engine, to launch any of the suggested webpage or search term, tap on it.

3. To go back to the previous webpage, tap the menu icon (the three dots icon, see the screenshot below) and tap on the back arrow. To go forward, tap the forward icon.

4. You can navigate web pages and get more done with following keys, which are explained below.

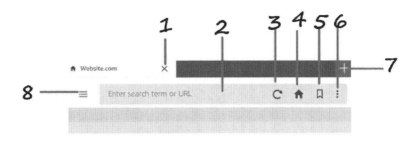

Number	Function
1.	Close a webpage
2.	URL input field
3.	Reload icon
4.	Home icon: Use this to go the home page.
5	Bookmark icon: Use this to add a webpage to your bookmark list
6	Menu icon: Use this to access features like **Forward & Backward buttons**, **Private browsing, Add/Remove bookmark, Share, Print, and Request desktop site, Find in Page.**
7	Add tab: Use this to add another browsing tab
8	Left Panel icon: Use this to access features like settings, bookmarks, and history.

Note: The **onscreen icons** may disappear and reappear depending on how you are using your tablet.

> ➢ **To open multiple pages/tabs**

You can open multiple pages on Silk browser and switch back and forth between them.

1. Open the browser by tapping on **silk browser icon**

2. Select '+' to open a new tab.

3. Type a web address into the URL field of the new tab and tap the search/go button (the arrow button on the virtual keyboard).

4. To switch back and forth between currently opened tabs, tap the small window directly on top of the webpage.

5. To close tab, select **X** icon.

Hint:

- To zoom in, place two fingers on the screen and spread them apart. To zoom out, move your two fingers closer together. Please note that not all webpages support zooming, but **you can force a page to zoom** (see page 36).

Bookmarking your favorite webpages

You can manually add bookmark if you know the web address of a web page.

> ➢ **To add a bookmark**

1. Tap on **silk browser icon** on the home screen.

2. Enter web address of the page you want to bookmark into the URL page and launch it.

3. Tap the bookmark icon (see the screenshot above).

4. Fill in the necessary field, if any. You can also tap on the menu icon and then tap on **Add bookmark** to add a bookmark.

6. To view your bookmarks, swipe from the left edge of the screen to open the left panel. Then tap on **Bookmarks**.

7. To edit a bookmark, swipe from the left edge of the screen to open the left panel and then tap on **Bookmarks.** Then tap on the particular bookmark you want to edit and enter the necessary information.

> **To access history**

1. Open silk web browser

2. Swipe from the left edge of the screen and tap on **History.**

3. Tap the X icon to delete individual webpages in the history.

4. To delete all the browsing history, tap the delete icon

5. Select all what you want to clear using the dialogue that appears and then tap **Clear.**

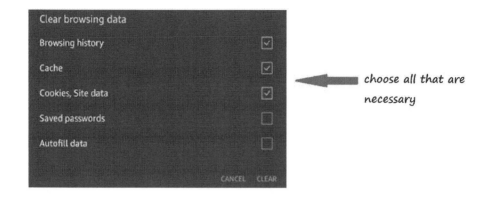

Clear browsing data

Browsing history ☑

Cache ☑

Cookies, Site data ☑

Saved passwords ☐

Autofill data ☐

CANCEL   CLEAR

choose all that are necessary

➢ **To load the desktop view of a webpage**

1. Tap on **silk browser icon** on home button.

2. Enter a web address into the URL page and launch it

3. Tap on **Menu** icon.

4. Tap on **Request desktop site.** To go back to the mobile site, select **Request mobile site.**

Hint: You may be unable to properly view some sites with flash contents in desktop mode, requesting mobile sites of websites like these may solve this problem.

➢ **Getting extra options on Silk browser**

There are still some options that are not present on the menu tab or the left panel. To access these options, open a webpage and tap and hold on a link, image file or video file on the webpage. Some of the options that may be available include **copy link URL, save image, open in a new tab, download link** among others.

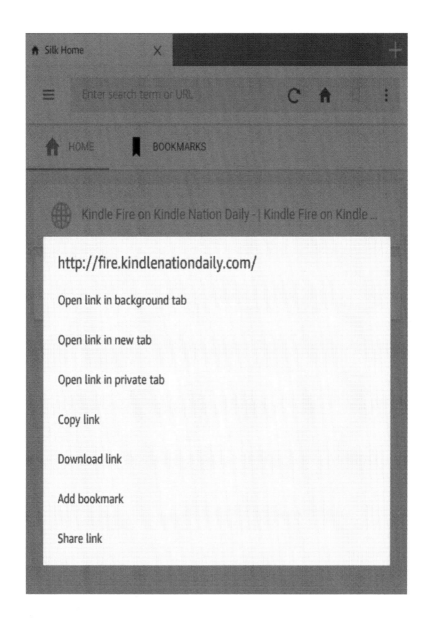

> ➢ **Downloading files and using the download folder**

The download folder contains your downloaded files and these may include documents file, video files, image files and webpages.

To access the download file, swipe from the left edge of the screen and tap on **Downloads.**

To download a file, click on this file and wait for the download to complete.

To download a link, image or video, tap and hold on the link/image/video and select the corresponding option.

Notes: The downloaded documents such as PDFs will be saved under **DOCS,** while downloaded images and videos will be saved under **PHOTOS.**

While trying to download a file, you may be prompted that the file might harm your device, tap **OK** to continue the downloading process if you are sure of the security of the file. If a file is downloading, it should show up in the notification bar, to access the notification bar, swipe down from the top of the screen.

> **Printing a webpage and saving it as PDF**

To print a webpage or save a webpage as PDF:

1. Tap the menu icon (the three dots icon located at the top right corner of the screen) and select **Print.** A dialog box will then appear for you to select a printer.

2. If you want to save the webpage as a PDF, select **Save as PDF** from the drop-down menu

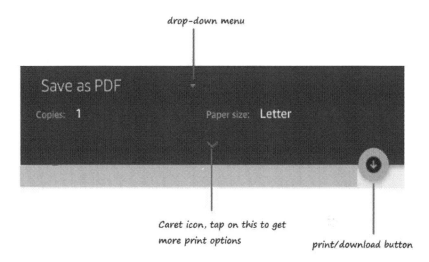

drop-down menu

Save as PDF

Copies: 1   Paper size: **Letter**

Caret icon, tap on this to get more print options

print/download button

3. Tap the download icon and then tap **Save.**
4. If you want to print a webpage, Fire tablet should be able to find your wireless printer and give you the option to add it. After adding your printer, use the caret icon to customize your printing. (Please make sure your device's Wi-Fi is On)
5. You will have the option to select those pages you want to print from the print preview that appears. To include/exclude a page, check the small box located at the lower left corner of the individual print page thumbnails.
6. When you are done, click on the download icon.

➢ **Managing the settings under Silk Browser**

1. Open the Silk Browser from the app grid.

2. Access the left panel and tap on **Settings** to view the following options:

Search Engine: This gives you the option to select Bing, Yahoo, or Google

Auto-Fill Form: This enables you to fill in information about yourself, and this information can then be used to fill online forms at later time.

Save Passwords: Use this option to save usernames and passwords for use on websites you visit most.

Accessibility:

Text Scaling: Use the slider to increase the size of the text in the box. Text should look this big after double-tapping on a paragraph when viewing a webpage.

Force Enable Zoom: When this option is selected, it overrides a website's request to prevent zooming.

Privacy: Use this to manage Silk browser Privacy settings.

Do Not Track – Use this setting to tell websites not to display ads based on your browsing or search history. However, please note that websites may choose to ignore these requests.

Clear Browsing Data: Use this option to delete your browser history, which include websites you've saved, saved passwords, and personal information added to forms.

Cloud Features: This option allows Silk browser to use the Amazon Cloud for faster web page loading with Instant Page Loads. Instant Page Load is a feature that predicts which web page you are going to access next and then preload it. It may make browsing experience faster but at the cost of data. If you really want to save data then this feature is better **Off.** Cloud features also allow Silk browser to support Flash video content using the Experimental Streaming Viewer.

Site Settings: Use this option to manage settings for websites visited in Silk browser. You have the option to manage settings for all sites or for individual sites. Under these settings, you can choose to enable or disable the following:

i. **Cookies:** These are small information (packets) stored on your browser to improve your browsing experience when using a site.

ii. **Location**: Use this option to allow sites to request access to your location. When a website wants to use your location data, Silk will prompt you at the bottom of the page. Tap **Allow** to send your location data to the website, or tap **Decline** to ignore the request.

iii. **Camera**: Use this option to allow sites to request use of the camera on your device.

iv. **Microphone:** Use this option to enable websites to make a request to use the microphone on your device.

v. **Notifications**: Use this option to manage website notification.

vi. **Images**: Use the option to prevent image from appearing on a site.

vii. **JavaScript:** Websites use JavaScript to improve the browsing experience. Please note that many sites will not function properly if this option is disabled.

viii. **Pop-ups:** Use this option to prevent pop-ups. Pop-ups are small windows that suddenly appear when you are browsing. Some pop-ups are actually wanted but some are just intruders.

ix. **Full Screen**: Use this option to manage full screen features on your browser.

About Silk: Use this option to get details about Silk browser.

Hint: If Silk browser starts misbehaving, try to clear the browsing data. To learn how to clear the browsing data, go to 30.

Using other Fire tablet apps

You can access any preinstalled app on your tablet by tapping its icon. You may be required to accept terms of service when using an app for the first time. To access more features on a particular app, swipe from the left edge of the screen to bring out left panel.

Communication

Using The Email App

To Setup an email

You may add more than one email account to your email app.
Note that your email is automatically sync with Calendar and
Contacts app on your tablet(unless this function is not
supported by your email provider).The email supports Gmail,
Yahoomail, Outlook etc.

1. From the Home screen, tap on **Email** app icon.
2. If you are using the Email app for the first time, enter your
   email address, and follow the onscreen instructions to
   connect your email accont.
3. If you have added one account and wish to add another email
   account, while in the Email app, swipe from the left edge of
   the screen and tap **Add Account,** and follow the onscreen
   instructions.
4. You can repeat the steps above to add another email account.

Note: If your email is not recognized, you will see the option to manually add your account using the advance setup screen. To manually add your account, you will need to obtain your email account information from your email provider.

I will advise that you contact your email provider or system administrator /in order to setup your email of Fire tablet.

To manage your email account

1. Tap on **Email** app icon from the app grid.
2. To compose email, tap the pen icon and the fill the address, subject and message sections. To add an attachment tap on the **attachment** icon (the clip icon). When done tap on **Send** icon.
3. To read email, tap on the email you want to read.
4. To reply a message, tap on the message and then tap on the **Reply** icon (the arrow-like icon).
5. To delete an email, while viewing an email tap **Delete** icon.
6. Use the search icon (magnifying lens icon) to search for specific emails in your inbox.
7. Tap the menu icon located at the upper part of the screen to get more options.

To download an attachment

Check for **paperclip** icon to know whether an email is having an attachment or not.

1. Tap on email app from the app grid screen
2. Tap on the message you want to open an attachment from, and scroll down to see the attachment.
3. Tap on the attachment and allow it download.
4. After the completion of the download, tap the **attachment** again to view the attachment.

Note: After saving an attachment, if the attachment is a photo or video, check your **Photos Library** to access it. If the attachment is a document, check the **Docs** library to access it.

Managing the email settings

Use this settings to customize your experience when using the email app.

Generally, there are four main tabs under email app settings and they are:

Email Settings: This option allows you to manage settings like message replies, attachments, email images, conversation settings among others.

Contact settings: This option allows you to manage contact settings.

Calendar settings: This option allows you to manage calendar settings.

Accounts: Tap on any account under this tab to manage settings like signature, default account, account name, account deletion among others.

Hint: Usually, you can get more information about a particular setting by reading the text under it.

Using Facebook and Twitter

You can link your device to Facebook or Twitter account to share your notes, photos, or book highlights. You can also imports contacts from Facebook account to your tablet.

To link a social account:

1. From **Settings,** tap **My Accounts,** and then tap **Social Networks.**
2. Then tap **Connect Your Twitter Account**, **Connect Your Facebook Account**, or **Goodreads**
3. Enter the account information for your social network, and then tap **Connect**.
4. Note that you can unlink your social account at any time.

Personal Information

Contacts

This app allows you to create and manage a list of your personal or business contacts. You can save names, mobile phone numbers, home phone numbers, email address, and more.

To create a contact

1. Tap on the contact app.

2. Tap on the icon located at the lower left corner of the screen.

3. Fill in the details and save the contact.

To manage a contact

1. Open the app grid and tap on **Contacts**

2. Tap on a contact from the list.

3. Use the onscreen icons to perform different tasks of your choice.

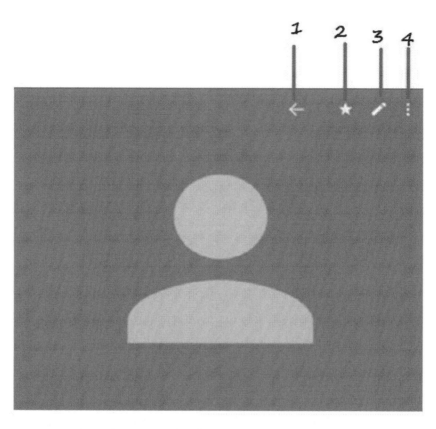

Number	Function
1.	Back icon
2.	Favorite icon: tap this to add a contact to your designate a person a VIP
3.	Tap this **pen icon** to change contact details.
4.	Tap **menu icon** to remove a contact or share a contact

Hint: from contact app, swipe from the left edge of the screen to get more options.

In addition, you can search the Contact app by tapping on the search button (the magnifying lens icon) located at the top of the screen.

Accessibility Features – The Special features for easy usage

Accessibility services are special features for those with physical challenges. It also provides you the opportunity to control your tablet in a special way.

VoiceView Demystified

VoiceView allows you to hear what is happening on the screen as you touch/interact with your screen.

To turn on the VoiceView

1. Swipe down from the top of the screen to access the Quick Actions panel, and then tap **Settings**.
2. Scroll down and tap on **Accessibility.**
3. Switch "On" the slider next to **VoiceView.**

To turn off the VoiceView

Note: Because the VoiceView is on, the first tap will select an item and you will then need to double-tap the screen to access the selected item or perform a specific action on the item.

1. Swipe down from the top of the screen with **two fingers** to open the **Quick Actions** panel, and then tap the **Settings** to select it.
2. Then double tap on the screen to open the settings menu.
3. Tap **Accessibility** to select it, and then double-tap the screen to open the Accessibility menu.
4. Tap **VoiceView** to select it, and then double tap the screen to open VoiceView options.
5. Next to the **VoiceViewReader**, tap the switch to select it, and then double-tap the screen to put off the VoiceView feature.
6. In the dialogue box that appears, tap **Continue** and then double tap the screen to confirm it.

Customizing the VoiceView

To customize the VoiceView when this feature is On:

1. Swipe down from the top of the screen with **two fingers** to open the **Quick Actions** panel, and then tap the **Settings** to select it.
2. Then double tap on the screen to open the settings menu.
3. Tap **Accessibility** to select it, and then double-tap the screen to open the Accessibility menu.
4. Tap **VoiceView** to select it, and then double tap the screen to open VoiceView options. The following options are available:
   - **Reading Speed**: Use this option to adjust the speed of the VoiceView voice.

- **VoiceView Volume:** Use this to set the volume level for the VoiceView voice. You can select Match device volume to use the physical volume keys on the device to adjust the volume for the VoiceView voice.

- **Feedback Tone Volume:** Use this to set the volume level for the feedback tone, or select Match device volume to use the physical volume keys on the device to adjust the volume for the feedback tone.

- **Key Echo:** Use this to determine what is echoed back to you while entering text. By default, characters are echoed as they are typed to confirm entry but this can be changed to **none, characters, words,** or **characters and words.**

- **Punctuation Level:** Use this to control what punctuation marks are read aloud to you.

Using the VoiceView

VoiceView allows you to navigate your tablet with some specific gestures. When this featured is activated, your tablet is able to recognizes shortcut gestures that help you quickly access menus and accessibility settings.

Note: To turn on the **VoiceView at any point in time (without going to the settings),** long press the power button until you hear an alert from your tablet, and then place two fingers (slightly apart) on the screen and hold it for five seconds. The following actions can be done when **VoiceView** is turned **on.**

1. **To go to the Home screen:** swipe your finger up then left in one stroke

2. **To go back to previous screen/page:** Swipe down and then left in one stoke with a finger.

3. **To open an item, icon or menu:** If you don't know (or cannot see) the location of the item, icon, or menu on the screen, swipe right or left using your finger until the name of that particular item you want to open is read to you and then double-tap on any part of the screen to open it. If you know (or can see) the location of item, icon, or menu on screen, drag your finger over that item (as if you want to gently clean the surface bearing that item with your finger) until the name of that item is read to you and then double-tap on any part of the screen to open/access it.

4. **To go to the next item/icon/menu on the screen:** Swipe down with your finger.

5. **To explore/select menus/items/icons on the screen:** Drag your finger over that item (as if you want to gently clean the surface bearing that item with your finger) until the name of that item is read to you.

6. **To move from one icon/item/menu to another on the screen:** swipe right or left using your finger until the name of that particular item you want to open is read to you.

Note: To move to the next item/icon/menu, swipe right or down using your finger. To move to the previous item/icon/menu, swipe left or up using a finger.

7. **To Open Quick Actions and Notifications Panel:** Swipe down from the top of the screen with **two fingers.**

8. **To open the left panel:** Swipe from left edge of the screen with two fingers.

9. **To open the category page:** Swipe from right edge of the screen with two fingers.

10. **Type on the keyboard:** slowly move a finger over the keys so that your tablet read the keys to you. When you hear the letter of your choice, lift up your finger to add the letter to what you are typing. You will hear a high-pitched tone when your finger strays outside the keyboard.

11. **To select a word from suggested word list:** Type a letter or few letters of a word, and then slide your finger from the bottom of screen until you hear a high-pitched tone. Without lifting your finger, then draw a circle in clockwise (direction) to hear a list of suggested words being read to you and then lift your finger to select the word when you hear the word of your choice. To move backwards through the words, draw circles counterclockwise.

12. **To Unlock the screen:** Swipe up from the bottom of the screen with two fingers.

Reading with VoiceView

VoiceView allows you to read books with certain gestures. When VoiceView is enabled, Text-to-Speech can automatically read your book and turn the pages for you when you open a book.

You can choose between continuous and non-continuous reading. Continuous reading will read all pages in the book to you, while non-continuous reading will read a page, character, or words on the page.

To show reading toolbar:

While reading, tap the screen, and then double-tap the screen to show the reading toolbar.

To start reading:

From the book you want to read, swipe down from the top of the page with two fingers. Make sure that the reading toolbar is not opened while doing this.

Switch from continuous to non-continuous reading

While reading, tap the screen to switch from reading continuously to non-continuous reading.

Change continuous reading speed

Tap the reading speed control to select it, and then double-tap the screen to change the reading speed. The continuous reading speed control is located at the bottom right corner of the screen when the reading toolbar is opened.

To change reading voice:

1. While the reading toolbar is opened, swipe down from the top of the screen with two fingers to open Quick Actions.
2. Then tap the **Settings** to select it.
3. Then double tap on the screen to open the settings menu.
4. Tap on **Keyboard & Language** to select it and then double tap to open the options under it.
5. Tap on **Text-to-Speech** to set a reading voice.

Note: Text-to-Speech voice can read in your device language. However, not all languages are supported.

Selecting text with VoiceView

Drag your finger across the screen to find the word you want to select. Double-tap the word, and then hold to listen to the definition of the word being read to you. To choose a highlight color or add a note; swipe to the left or right.

Read one page, paragraph, character, or a word at a time

You can command VoiceView to read one page, paragraph, character, or a word at a time. To do this:

1. Using your finger, swipe up and then right in a single stroke to activate the **Local Context Menu**.
2. Then select your preferred reading level.

Note: Some reading level options may unavailable depending on the book being read.

To open the "Go To" menu

Using two fingers, swipe from the left edge of the screen, and then double-tap a chapter or section.

To turn a page

Using two fingers, swipe left with to go to the next page or swipe right to go to the previous page.

Screen Magnifier

This option allows you to use certain gestures to magnify your screen so that you may better see what is on the screen.

To turn on screen magnifier

1. Swipe down from the top of the screen to access the Quick Actions panel, and then tap **Settings**.
2. Scroll down and tap on **Accessibility.**
3. Tap the switch next to **Screen Magnifier** and then tap **OK.**

When the Screen magnifier is on, you can perform any of these actions:

i. Zoom in: triple tap on the screen with a finger. If you just want to temporarily magnify the screen, triple tap on the screen with a finger and hold, to see other parts of the screen, drag your finger across the screen.

ii. Pan: Place two fingers slightly apart on the screen and then drag it across the screen.

iii. To zoom in or out after activating Screen magnifier: Use your two fingers to pinch inward or outward until you get the magnification of your choice.

iv. Turn on Screen Magnifier during device setup: Press the Power button until "Do you want to shut down your Fire?" appears on the screen, and then triple-tap the screen and hold your finger on the screen for five seconds.

Using the Braille with Fire HD 8 Tablet

You can use a braille device with your Fire tablet but you will need to install BrailleBack app. This app is available on Amazon appstore. After installing the app, please follow the steps below to pair your Braille device with Fire tablet (assuming that VoiceView is disabled):

1. Swipe down from the top of the screen to access the Quick Actions panel, and then tap **Bluetooth** and enable it.
2. Then tap **Pair With Bluetooth Device.**
3. Locate the name of your braille device.
4. Tap on the name and then follow the onscreen instructions to finish the setup.

You can adjust the output settings of your braille so as to get better performance. To do this:

1. Swipe down from the top of the screen to access the Quick Actions panel, and then tap **Settings**.
2. Scroll down and tap on **Accessibility.**
3. Under **Service**, tap **BrailleBack**

4. Tap **On** and then tap **OK.**

5. Then tap on **Configure BrailleBack** and select your preferred output setting from the list.

Note: Instructions giving above are based on the assumption that VoiceView is disabled. If VoiceView is enabled, you will need to follow slightly different steps to pair your braille device. For example, if the VoiceView is enabled, you will need to swipe down from the top of the screen with **two fingers** to open the **Quick Actions** panel. In addition, when the VoiceView is on, any first tap will only select an item and you will then need to double-tap the screen to access the selected item or perform a specific action on the item. Please refer to the section on **VoiceView** (see page 47) to learn more.

Managing The Hearing Settings

Hearing settings are features that enable you to customize sound settings.

To convert Stereo to mono

1. Swipe down from the top of the screen to access the Quick Actions panel, and then tap **Settings**.

2. Scroll down and tap on **Accessibility.**

3. Under the **Hearing Settings**, Tap the switch next to **Convert Stereo to Mono** to disable the stereo sound.

Note: Disabling the stereo sound enables you to play all audio in a single channel, this is especially important if you have hearing aid in one ear or you are using a single ear bud.

Enabling Closed Captioning

Closed captioning is a feature that allows hearing impaired individual have a visual display (usually in form of text) of audio portion of a program. It can be likened to subtitling. For those videos that have close captioning enable, you should be able to view the closed captioning of those videos while watching it on Amazon Instant Video. Look out for **CC** icon when searching for videos on Amazon Instant Videos to know whether they support close captioning. You can also access closed captioning feature on your Silk browser. To customize closed captioning to your taste, visit **www.amazon.com/cc**

1. Swipe down from the top of the screen to access the Quick Actions panel, and then tap **Settings**.
2. Scroll down and tap on **Accessibility.**
3. Under the **Hearing Settings**, Tap the switch next to **Closed Captioning.**

To customize Closed Captions

1. Repeat the first three steps above

2. Tap **Closed Captioning Preferences** to customize your settings for:

- **Text**: Use this to adjust text size, color, opacity, font, and edge style.

- **Text Background**: Use this to select the color and opacity for the text's background.

- **Window Background**: Use this to select the color and opacity for the Closed Captioning window.

3. If you want to use the settings you selected for Closed Captioning on Amazon Video captions, tap **On** next to **Use Amazon web settings for Amazon Video captions**.

4. To reset to defaults settings, tap **Reset to Defaults**.

TOOLS

Amazon FreeTime Demystified

Amazon FreeTime allows you to create individual profiles for your children and customize a reading goal for them. As a parent, you have the opportunity to track the reading progress of your children. Kids earn achievements in form of rewards that help them keep track of their personal reading accomplishments. When Amazon FreeTime is active, access to Kindle Store, the Silk Browser, Goodreads, in-app purchases and Social media features are automatically blocked so that your kids can't access them. In addition, children can only read only books added to their library.

How set-up Amazon FreeTime

1. Swipe down from the top of the screen to access the Quick Actions panel, and then tap **Settings**.
2. Tap on **Profiles & Family Library.**
3. Tap **Add a child profile**. Note that if you have not done so before, you will need to setup lock screen PIN/password in order for your child to use Amazon FreeTime.

4. Select **Choose a profile picture** to add a profile picture.

5. Enter your child's name, birthdate, and gender, and then select between **Use Amazon FreeTime** (for children ages eight and younger) or **Use Teen Profile** (for children ages nine and older).

6. Tap **Add Profile,** and follow the onscreen instruction to add content to your child's profile. You can create up to four profiles.

7. Tap **Done** to save all the settings and create a new profile.

Hint: To access your child's profile after you have set it up, swipe down form the top of the screen to access Quick Actions panel. You can also access it from the Amazon FreeTime app or from the lock screen.

Note: If you select **Amazon FreeTime profile**, the screen orientation is automatically locked to landscape view.

In addition, you may also subscribe to Amazon FreeTime Unlimited. Amazon FreeTime Unlimited is an optional monthly subscription for Amazon FreeTime that offers thousands of books for smaller children.

How to manage Amazon FreeTime Profile

1. Swipe down from the top of the screen to access the Quick Actions panel, and then tap **Settings**.

2. Tap on **Profiles & Family Library** and tap your child's name.

3. Tap on **Daily Goals & Time Limits.** Then adjust the settings you like:

    a) **Weekdays / Weekends**: Use this option to choose different educational goals and time limits for the weekend or weekday.

    b) **Bedtime**: Use this option to set a time limit for when your child can use Amazon FreeTime during the day. Use the **Turn off by** setting to set the time when Amazon FreeTime is turned off. Use the **Stay off until** setting to set the time when Amazon FreeTime can be used again.

    c) **Educational Goals**: Use this option to set goals for viewing educational content. Use the dropdown menus to choose the amount of time you want your child to view contents. Tap the checkbox next to **Learn First** to prevent non-educational content from being used until your child's goals are met.

    d) **Total Screen Time**: Use this option to limit the total time your child can spend in Amazon FreeTime.

    e) **Time by Activity**: Use this option to specify individual time limits for specific activities done while using Amazon FreeTime. To choose unlimited time, move the bar to the far right. To block access to a particular content, move the bar to the far left.

How to add your content to a profile in Amazon FreeTime

One of the beauties of Amazon FreeTime is that you can add exactly what you want included in your child's profile. You have the option to add book, videos, and apps to your child profile. To add content to a profile:

1. Swipe down from the top of the screen to access the Quick Actions panel, and then tap **Settings**.
2. Tap on **Profiles & Family Library** and tap your child's name.
3. Tap **Add Content** and select a content type.
4. Select the items/titles you want by checking them. You may also remove a title by unchecking the title.
5. Tap **Done.**

Hint: If you don't know what to add to your child's profile, you can tap on **Kid-Friendly** to view recommended titles in your library (powered by Amazon).

Notes:

1. Not all books can be added to a child's profile. Personal documents, audiobooks, Prime videos, and music may not be added to a profile. However, Amazon made it known that public library books or books borrowed from the Kindle Owner's Lending Library or from Kindle Unlimited can be added to a child's profile. But these books will be unavailable in your child's profile when they are returned or removed from your library.

2. Removing a book from a child's library does not remove it from your device unless you remove the book by selecting **Remove from Device** option.

Using a Profile in Amazon FreeTime

1. To launch a profile, open the Amazon FreeTime app and tap on the profile you want to open. If you are in a lock screen, tap the profile icon in the upper right corner of the screen and then tap the profile you want to open. Then swipe up from the bottom of the screen.

2. To Exit Amazon FreeTime, from the child's profile, swipe down from the top of the screen and tap **Exit Profile.**

3. To open a title, from the Home categories menu (located at the top of the screen), tap on a content library (e.g **Books**). When in a content library, tap a title to open it.

4. To search for content in a child's profile, from the Home categories menu (located at the top of the screen) tap **Characters** and then search by popular character or theme.

5. To pin an item as favorite, tap and hold the item and select **Add to Home.** Pinning favorite items make it easier to find an item on home screen.

6. To track daily progress of a child, from the Home categories menu (located at the top of the screen), tap a content library and then tap **Progress** icon (a badge-like icon). This enables you to see how much time your child has left to complete

their reading goal, and how much time left until **Bedtime** will appear.

7. To navigate contents, swipe left or right.

Hint: By default, your child is allowed to take pictures using the camera on your tablet, to disable this option:

1. Swipe down from the top of the screen to access the Quick Actions panel, and then tap **Settings**.
2. Tap on **Profiles & Family Library** and tap your child's profile.
3. Then swipe down from the top of the screen and tap **Settings**, enter your lock screen pin.
4. Tap the switch next to **Enable Camera and Photo Gallery** to turn it off.

Editing a Profile

1. Swipe down from the top of the screen to access the Quick Actions panel, and then tap **Settings**.
2. Tap on **Profiles & Family Library** and tap the child's profile name you want to edit.
3. Tap **Edit profile.**

Removing a profile

4. To remove a child's profile, swipe down from the top of the screen to access the Quick Actions panel, and then tap **Settings**.

5. Tap on **Profiles & Family Library** and tap the child's profile name you want to remove.

6. Then tap on **Remove from household** and tap **Remove Profile.**

Understanding Amazon Household and Family Library

Amazon Household is a feature that allows you to have joint Amazon account with another adult to be able to jointly manage up to four Amazon FreeTime child profiles. Amazon Household typically comprises two adults and up to four children. Amazon Household is accompanied by a feature called Family Library which lets you share books with each other across Amazon devices and Kindle apps.

Note: Your annotations, most recent page read, and last page read in books are not affected when you share books with other Household members. That is, each adult will keep separate furthest page read locations, notes, highlights, and social media accounts.

To set-up or add an adult to your household:

1. Swipe down from the top of the screen to access the Quick Actions panel, and then tap **Settings**.

2. Tap on **Profiles & Family Library** and tap **Add Adult**.

3. You will then need to give your device to the adult you would like to add to your household to enable him/her to enter his/her Amazon account details. You may not need to give your device to the other individual if you know his/her account details. If the other individual does not have an Amazon account, then that person must create one by visiting Amazon website in order to continue the set-up process.

4. After entering the account details, the person will have the option to enable sharing. The person you are adding may choose if he/she wants to share all his/her purchased books or just individual books. Note that when the person you are adding choose to enable sharing, he/she is authorizing you to use credit cards associated with his/her Amazon account for purchase on Amazon. It is important that you explain this information to whoever you are adding to avoid any unnecessary surprises.

5. When you are done entering this details tap **Continue.**

6. The person you are adding will be prompted to give you back your device to continue the set-up process. You will then be given the choice to enable sharing also. You can choose if you want to share all your purchased books or just individual books with the person you added. Note that if you choose to enable sharing, you are authorizing the second adult to use

credit cards associated with your Amazon account for purchase on Amazon.

Notes:

- Family library will not be set up if either adult (i.e. you or the second adult) declines to enable content sharing. However, the second adult will still be added to your household and the management of child profiles with Amazon FreeTime will be shared with the two adults.

To set-up household profile and create family library using the Amazon website:

1.   Launch www.amazon.com/mycd from your browser.

2.   Click on **Settings** tab, and locate **Households and Family Library**.

3.   From Households and Family Library, click on **Invite an Adult.**

4.   Follow the onscreen instructions and click on **Verify Account** or **Create a New Account**.

5.   Both adults will be asked to share their payments methods and services in order to share content. Click on **We authorize payment sharing** if you agree to share the information, and then click on **Create Household**.

6.   Each adult will have the opportunity check or uncheck the content types they want to share. You may also decide what to share later.

7.   Choose **Create Your Family Library** when you are done. Please note that if you choose **We don't authorize payment sharing** in step 5, then content will not be shared between the two adults in the Amazon Household. However, management of child profiles with Amazon FreeTime will be shared with the two adults.

To manage which devices can view shared content:

If you enable content sharing, you can choose which device gets access to shared content by following the instructions below:

1. Swipe down from the top of the screen and tap **Settings**, and then tap **Profiles & Family Library**.
2. Tap the partner's profile name, and then tap **Select Devices That Show...... Content.**
3. Then select the devices or Kindle reading apps that you want to allow to access shared content.

Creating a child profile in your household

You can create up to four child profiles in your household and choose which content is shared with them. Note that if you have already created up to four Amazon FreeTime child profile as described in the preceding section, then you may skip these steps because they will be automatically added to your Household.

Creating a child profile in your household on your device is similar to what was described in the preceding section.

To create a child profile in your household from the Amazon website:

1. Launch www.amazon.com/mycd from your browser.

2. Click on **Settings** tab, and locate **Households and Family Library**.

3. From Households and Family Library, click on **Add Child**.

4. Fill in the child details and then select **Add Child Profile**.

Removing an Account from Household

For one reason or the other, you may choose to remove an adult account from your household. However, if you remove an adult account from household or an adult voluntarily leaves your household, neither you nor the second adult will be able to link another adult account or join another household within a period of 180 days.

To remove an adult account from your household:

1. Swipe down from the top of the screen to access the Quick Actions panel, and then tap **Settings**.
2. Tap on **Profiles & Family Library** and tap the adult's profile you want remove.
3. Then tap on **Remove from household.**

To remove an adult account from your household on Amazon website:

1. Launch www.amazon.com/mycd from your browser.

2. Click on **Settings** tab, and locate **Households and Family Library**.

3. From Households and Family Library, locate the adult profile you want to remove and hover the mouse over it or click on it (if necessary), and then click **Leave Household** or **Remove from household** from the options. Then click on **Remove Adult**.

Note that child profiles are unaffected by the removal of an adult account from a household. Child profiles will remain with the account that did not leave the household. To delete a child's profile, please follow the instructions in the preceding section.

In addition, most settings on your Fire tablet only affects your profile, however, settings like Wi-Fi, language, date and time, and parental controls affect all the profiles on your device.

A Comprehensive Guide on Reading Books on Your Device

One of the top things you will probably be using your tablet to do is reading and I will like to really talk about it at length in this section.

Reading a book

To read a book:

1. Tap on the book category on the home screen.
2. Select any book from your library to read or search for a new book.
3. Swipe from left edge of the screen to access left panel to navigate menus.
4. You may move between pages by swiping your finger across the screen.

Hint: To view more options on a book without opening it, tap and hold on the book's cover and select an option of your choice.

To zoom a page while reading:

1. While on the book's app page, tap on the book title to access the book.

2. When on the page you want to read, place your two fingers on the screen and slowly spread them apart to zoom in until you get your desired font size. To zoom out, pinch your two fingers together.

To change the fonts, margins, line spacing, or background color of a book:

1. While on a page of the book you want to read, tap on the center of the screen to bring the out the toolbar.

2. Then tap on **Aa** icon located upper right section of the screen.

3. To adjust screen brightness, drag the slider to right or left.

4. To change the font size, tap + or – next to **Font Size.**

5. To change the font, tap the current font name and then select a font. If available, you may also select publisher font. Not all books support this.

6. To change the background color, tap the small drop-down arrow next to **Color** and then select a color.

7. To change the margins, tap the small drop-down arrow next to **Margins,** and choose from the available options.

8. To change the line spacing, tap the small drop-down arrow next to **Line Spacing,** and pick the line spacing of your choice.

9. When you are done, tap the outside of the dialog box.

Navigating pages of a book

To go to the next or previous page in a book:

1. Open the book of your choice by tapping on the cover or the title of the book from the books app page.
2. Tap the right side of the screen to go the next page or tap the left side of the screen to go to the previous page.
3. Alternatively, you may swipe towards left with your finger to go to the next page or swipe toward right to go to the previous page.
4. To quickly move through pages, tap the center of the screen to bring the reading progress bar into view and then drag small circle on the reading progress bar to quickly move across different pages of the book. The reading progress bar is the long bar at the lower part of the screen which shows your location in a book and the percentage of the book you have read.
5. To go to a specific location of a book, tap the center of the book you are reading to bring out the reading toolbar. Then tap the menu icon located at the top left corner of the screen and then tap **Go to.** Enter a location and tap **Go.**

Syncing to furthest page read

You can sync to the furthest page read across your device by tapping the center of the book you are reading to bring out the reading toolbar. Then tap the menu icon located at the top left corner of the screen and tap **Sync.**

X-Ray feature

X-Ray allows you to get more information about the book you are reading. With X-Ray feature, you can view notable clips, images, terms and people right from the page you are in a book. This feature allows you to see all the passages in book that mention a particular term, places, topics, historical figures, and many more.

Downside: Unfortunately, this feature is not available in all books present on Amazon. In fact, several thousands of books on Amazon don't have this feature enabled. If you want to know whether a book has X-Ray enabled or not, go to the product description of the book on Kindle store.

To access the X-Ray feature:

1. When you are on a particular page of a book, press and hold on a character's name or place mentioned to bring out the smart lookup card.
2. If the X-Ray is available for the book, you should see X-Ray results displayed alongside the Wikipedia and Dictionary results on the smart lookup card. You may need to swipe left or right to move across the cards. To get more information on a particular character, tap **More on Shelfari** (if the option is available).

Hint: If you come across a new term, name of a person or place, then try checking if there is X-Ray result for it. This allows you to see different locations in the book containing that particular term or name of a place. To check any word for X-Ray, follow the step mentioned above.

Note that X-Ray feature may not extend its search beyond the furthest page read in a book. Tap to show all excerpts when you get to your furthest page read in order to ensure that you get X-Ray results for a whole book.

To get access to more comprehensive X-Ray results while reading, please follow the steps below:
1. While reading, tap the center of the screen to display the reading toolbar.
2. Then tap on the three vertical dots icon (menu icon) located at the top right corner of the screen. Then tap on **X-Ray.**

You may also be able to tap the **X-Ray** icon without first tapping then menu icon.

3. If the book has the X-Ray enabled, then a dialog box will appear. Generally, the dialog box should contain the X-Ray results for people, places, term and notable clips.

Note that it may be just three tabs in some cases, because the image tab may be missing in books that have no image in them.

i.   Notable Clip: This tab contains notable passages/scenes in a book

ii.   People: This tab generally contains the names of people featured in the book. Under this tab, you can sort your X-Ray results by Relevance or Alphabetically.

iii.   Term: This tab typically contains the names of places, historical figures etc. Under this tab, you can sort your X-Ray results by Relevance or Alphabetically.

iv.   Image: This tab allows you to flip through the images in a book.

While reading any book that supports X-Ray feature, tap on any tab mentioned above to check the details under each of them.

Blue Shade

Blue shade gives a special bluish color to the screen of your tablet. When used at night, this feature is claimed to be able to suppress production of sleep-promoting melatonin and therefore it may help you stay wake longer.

To turn Blue Shade on/off:

- Swipe down from the top of the screen and tap **Blue Shade**.

To adjust Blue Shade settings:

- Swipe down from the top of the screen and select Settings.
- Tap **Display**, and then tap **Blue Shade**. Use the slider bars to control the screen brightness and color. Using the slider bars, you move between **red candle light** and **yellow moonlight**.
- Turn on **Automatic Activation** if you want Blue Shade to gradually turn on in the evening and gradually off at sunrise.

Sharing a text/passage

You can share what you are reading with friends by using the Share button. Using this share feature makes it very easy to quickly share a book with love ones so that they can also get a copy of the book. This is because a link to the book is usually automatically included when you share a portion of a book. To share a note or a highlight:

1. Tap and drag to select what you want to share, and then choose Share from the dialog box that appears.
2. Follow the onscreen instruction to complete this process.

Bookmarking a Page

You can bookmark those pages of a book that interest you most. You may also use the bookmark feature to know the place where you stopped reading.

To bookmark a page:

1. While on the page you want to bookmark, tap the top right corner of the screen to bring bookmark button into view and add a page to bookmarks.

2. To remove the bookmark, tap on the Bookmark button icon ▮ (located at the top right corner of the screen).

3. To manage your bookmarks, tap the center of the screen to bring the reading toolbar into view, and then tap the **Bookmarks** icon.

Managing highlights

Just as we use marker to shade interesting passages in a book, you can also shade those passages in a book that are important to you by highlighting them.

To highlight a text/passage:

1. While reading a book, tap and drag across the words you want to highlight.

2. Choose a color.

Tip: If you want to highlight a large passage that runs into another page, tap and drag across the words you want to highlight, the page will automatically turn when you get to the bottom right corner of the screen. You can continue like this to select more pages of a book.

To delete your highlights in a book:

1. Open the book and locate the highlight you want to delete.

2. Press and hold a word in the highlighted area, tap **X** icon located on the color previously selected.

Hints: To edit a highlight, follow the above steps to delete the highlight and then reselect appropriate text you want to include in the highlight and tap on Highlight.

To change the highlight color, press and hold a word in the highlighted area and select another color from the dialog box that appears.

To turn on/off Popular Highlights:
1. Tap the center of the screen to bring the reading toolbar into view, and then tap the menu icon ⁞ located at the upper right corner of the screen.
2. Tap **Additional Settings**.
3. Tap the switch next to Popular Highlights to turn it on or off.

Hint: Popular highlights are usually marked by dashed underline. You can check for this when reading.

Managing notes

Notes are the text you type, this is similar to jotting notes in the margins of a printed book.

To add a note to a text/passage:

1. While reading a book, tap and drag across the words you want to add a note to.

2. Tap the **Note** ▇ icon, and then type your note.

3. Tap **Save** to create your note. A small notepad appears in the text where you made the note.

To edit your notes:

1. Tap the notepad ▤ icon where the note appears.

2. Make necessary changes.

3. Tap **Save** when you are done.

To delete your notes in a book:

1. Tap the notepad ▤ icon where the note appears.

2. Tap **Delete**.

Hint: You can share your notes from a Kindle textbook, to do this, tap the center of the book to bring the reading toolbar into view, and then tap **Notes** icon. Then tap the **Share** icon and tap **Export** to send it as an attachment in an email.

Dictionary

The language you choose when setting up your device will determine the dictionary that shows up when using your device. However, you may change your default language at any time.

Please note that changing the Language of your device will also change the default dictionary language. To learn more about changing the device language, please refer to page 15.

To access Dictionary:

1. While reading a book, tap and hold on a word and swipe right (if necessary) until Dictionary dialogue box is brought into view.
2. Tap **Full Dictionary** to see more information about the word you are viewing.
3. Tap **Change Dictionary** to select another dictionary.

Please note that you may be asked to download a dictionary before you can use it.

Wikipedia

Your device comes with Wikipedia feature. This feature allows you to look up words in Wikipedia (an online free encyclopedia).

To access Wikipedia:

1. While reading a book, tap and hold on a word and swipe right or left (if necessary) until Wikipedia dialogue box is brought into view.

2. To learn more about a word or a phrase, tap **Go to Wikipedia.**

Translation

You can translate words from one language to another on your device.

1. While reading a book, tap and hold on a word and swipe right (if necessary) until Translation dialogue box is brought into view.

2. To change the Language you want to translate to, tap on it.

3. To hear the translated text, tap the speaker button.

Using the Flashcards

You can access flashcards when reading some books (textbooks).

1. Tap the center of the book to bring reading toolbar into view.

2. Tap **Flashcards**

3. To create flashcards, tap + icon and enter necessary details.

4. To edit flashcards, tap the pen icon and enter necessary details.

5. To rename a set of flashcards, tap and hold the set and select **Rename.**

6. To delete flashcards, tap the pen icon and then tap the delete icon. To delete a set of flashcard, tap and hold the set and select **Delete.**

7. To add a new flashcard to a set, tap the ⊕ icon.

8. To manage a set of flashcard, tap the set and then tap a flashcard in the set to read the information on the other side of the card. If the answer is correct, drag the flashcard into the **Correct** [✓] box, if not, drag it into **Incorrect** [✗] box.

9. To reshuffle a set, tap ⤬ icon

10. To restart a set, tap ⟲ icon

Word Wise

Word Wise feature on your Fire tablet makes it easy to view meanings of complex words without need to look words up. This feature is really beneficial for small kids. It also makes learning old English words easier.

Downside: Not all books have Word Wise enabled. You can know if a book has Word Wise feature enabled by checking the product description page of the book in Kindle store.

To turn on or turn off Word Wise:

1. Tap the center of the screen to bring the reading toolbar into view, and then tap the menu icon ⋮ in the upper right corner of the screen.
2. Tap **Word Wise** and enable it.

To manage Word Wise

When Word Wise feature is on for an enabled title, your device automatically displays simple meanings of difficult words. Tap on any of these words to learn more about them.

Using the Word Runner

Word runner allows you to read books without moving your look. With this feature, you can easily fix your look at the center of the screen.

To use Word Runner:

1. Tap the center of the screen to bring reading toolbar into view, and then tap the menu icon ⋮ in the upper left corner.
2. Tap **Word Runner.**
3. Tap the play icon located at the button of the page you are reading.

4. Use the slider at the button of the screen to adjust the speed of Word Runner. You can choose between 100 to 900 words per minute.

5. To pause Word Runner to quickly do some things, tap and hold the screen. To continue using Word Runner, just remove your finger from the screen. You can also tap on the pause icon to pause this feature. When you are done, tap on the play icon.

6. To reread a sentence while using Word Runner, tap the pause icon, and then tap the forward/backward icons to move through sentences. When you are done, tap the play button to continue reading at the new location.

7. To exit Word Runner, tap the **X** icon and then tap the arrow icon located at the top left corner of the screen.

Please note that you may not be able to view images while using Word Runner. It appears that images are not supported on Word Runner. May be this will supported in the future. You can tap the **X** icon to quickly view images in a book while using Word Runner.

Word Runner will tell you your reading speed when you complete a chapter and this can help you know how fast you are at reading.

Using Text-to-Speech

If you don't have audiobook of a book but you an eBook version, you can try using the text-to-speech feature.

You can know if a book has Text-to-Speech feature enabled by checking the product description page of the book in Kindle store.

To use Text-to-Speech feature:

1. Tap the center of the screen to bring reading toolbar into view, and then tap the menu icon ⋮ located at the upper right corner of the screen.
2. Tap **Additional Settings**
3. Tap **On** next to Text-to-Speech.
4. While reading the book, tap the center of the screen to bring reading toolbar into view, and then tap on play icon
5. To adjust the reading speed, tap speed ☻ icon.
6. If you are reading a book in another language, you will have the option to download the Text-to-Speech voice for this language. The download button is usually located at the bottom of Text-to-Speech progress bar.

Creating schedules and more with the Calendar

Your tablet provides you with a **calendar** app to help you organize your schedules and tasks more conveniently and effectively. You can create schedules and add events.

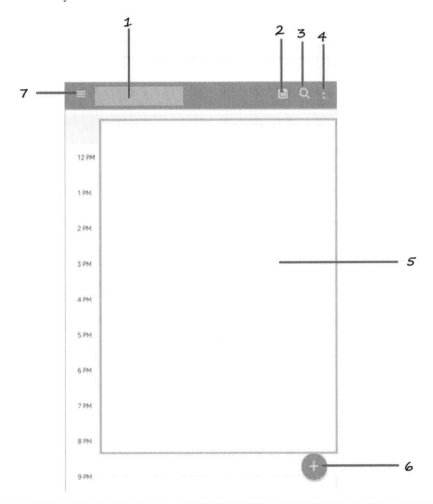

Number	Function
1.	Date field
2.	Day view icon
3.	Use this icon to search your calendar
4.	**Menu icon:** Use this to access agenda, day view, week view or month view
5.	Time/Day field
6.	Tap this icon to add an event
7.	Tap this to bring out the left panel

> ➤ **To create an event**

1. Open the application grid and tap on **Calendar.**

2. Tap on the '**+**' icon at right lower side of the screen and enter the details.

3 When you are finished, tap checkmark to save the event.

> ➤ **To view an event/schedule**

1. Open the application gird and tap on **Calendar**

2. If the calendar is set to display **Day** view, the calendar app automatically displays the events for the day.

3. Then tap on an event to view.

> ➤ **To change calendar view**

1. Open the application grid and tap on **Calendar**

2. Tap the menu icon (the three vertical dots icon) to switch between **List, Day, Week and Month Views.**

> ➤ **To edit or delete an event**

1. Open the application grid and tap on **Calendar**

2. If the calendar is set to display **Day** view, the calendar app automatically displays the events for the day.

3. Tap the event.

4. Tap the menu icon (shown in the screenshot above) and then tap the **Edit** icon

4. To delete an event, tap the event and then tap the **Delete** icon.

> ➤ **To View or Hide Calendars**

If you have multiple calendars (calendars from Yahoo mail, Facebook etc.) synced to your tablet you can select which ones to display.

1. Open the application grid and tap on **Calendar.**

2. Swipe from the left edge of the screen, and then tap the checkbox next to the calendar you want to display.

Hint: To customize your calendar even more, swipe from the left edge of the screen and tap on **Settings.**

Managing your document with ' Docs'

Docs is an app that allows you to easily access documents present on your tablet. You should also be able to view document that you transfer from your PC under this app. *Note:* Not all formats of document are supported. The supported document formats include PDF, unprotected MOBI, PRC natively, DOC, DOCX, Kindle (AZW), KF8, TXT

➢ **To access your documents**

1. From the home screen, tap on **DOCS** on the app grid

2. To print a document, press and hold the document want to print and select **Print**

3. To send a document to your device, swipe right from the edge of the screen and tap on **Add Docs to your Library** and then follow the onscreen instructions.

4. To view a document, tap on the document you want to view.

Hint: To enjoy viewing large pdf files, I will advise you download official PDF application from Amazon Appstore. In addition, **WPS Office + PDF** app is good for viewing and editing documents and you may consider downloading it from Amazon Appstore.

In addition, please note that your Fire tablet only support wireless printing.

To learn more about how to send a document to your device using Send-to-Kindle option, please refer to page 139.

Connectivity

PC Connections

Your tablet can be connected to a PC with USB cable. This will enable you to transfer files such as audio files, video files, document files and image files to your tablet from your PC.

Warning: Do not disconnect the USB cable from a computer while the device is transferring or accessing data. This may result in data loss or damage to your tablet.

Note: Personal content transferred to your Amazon Fire Tablet is stored on your device and not stored in Amazon cloud. However, if your settings allows, image files and video files may be automatically backed up when connected to Wi-Fi.

Transferring content via USB

1. Connect your device to a PC with a USB cable. Your Fire tablet should appear in the same location as external USB drives usually appear. For Windows users, this is typically under "My Computer" menu.

2. Open the Amazon Fire drive so as to see the different folders present. Tap on **Internal storage** to see different folder such

as **Books**. Note that you may not be able to access the folders if your tablet is locked.

3. To transfer files from your PC to your tablet. Locate the file you want to transfer on your PC and click and then drag and drop the file into corresponding folders on your Tablet. For example books should be dragged to **Books** folder.

4. Safely eject your tablet from your PC.

5. Launch the corresponding content library on your tablet to see the transferred files. For example, image files will be located under the device tab of **Photos.**

Note: After the transfer, your transferred files should appear under the corresponding content library on your device:

- Video files should be under Photos
- Image files should be under Photos
- Audio files should appear under Music library
- Book should appear under the Books library
- Personal documents should be under Docs library

Note: Note that your tablet will only recognize the files you transferred if the file is a supported file type. I will advise that you download **ES File Explorer** from Amazon Appstore so as to have real time control of the files on your tablet.

In addition, Mac users will need to download a file transfer app from **www.android.com/filetransfer** in order to be able to transfer files from their computer to Fire tablet.

Note: If you do factory reset to your tablet, you will need to re-transfer the files again.

Hint: You can download your purchased books to your computer by following these steps:

1. Go to **www.amazon.com/mycd**
2. Tap on **My Contents** tab and tap on small action box next to the title you want to download
3. Select **Download & Transfer via USB**

Wi-Fi

Using your tablet, you can connect to the internet or other network devices anywhere an access point or wireless hotspot is available.

To activate the Wi-Fi feature and connect to a network

1. Swipe down from the top of the screen to open the quick actions menu, and then tap **Settings**.
2. Tap on **Wireless**
3. Tap **Wi-Fi**
4. Tap the switch next to **Wi-Fi** to turn it **on.**
5. You may also manually add network by tapping **Join Other Networks**.
6. Select a network under Wi-Fi network.
7. Enter a password for the network (if necessary).
8. Tap **Connect.**

Note:

- The Wi-Fi feature running in the background will consume battery. To save battery, put it off whenever you are not using.
- Tap the menu icon (the three vertical dots icon located at the top right corner of the screen) to access more Wi-Fi options.
- After you connect to a Wi-Fi network, your device should connect automatically to it again whenever that network is in range.
- The Wi-Fi may not connect a network if the network signal is not very good.
- If your device can't connect to a wireless network, check if the airplane mode is on. If the airplane mode is off and you can't still connect to a wireless network, try restarting your router or your tablet or both.

Tip: To disable all connections, turn **on** the **airplane mode** by swiping down from the top of the screen of your tablet and tapping on the **Airplane Mode**.

When Wi-Fi is active, **Wi-Fi** icon 📶 is displayed on the status bar.

Access More By Using Bluetooth

Bluetooth option allows you to connect to another Bluetooth device within range

Note: If there are obstacles, the operating distance of the Bluetooth may be reduced.

To use Bluetooth feature:

1. Swipe down from the top of the screen to open the quick actions menu, and then tap **Settings**.
2. Tap on **Wireless**
3. Tap **Bluetooth**
4. Then tap the switch next to **Bluetooth.** The switch then turns orange to signify that your device is discoverable.
5. Tap **Pair a Bluetooth Device.**
6. Select a device to connect with.

7. When connected, a **Bluetooth icon** will appear next to the **Wi-Fi icon,** if the Bluetooth icon is grey then the device and your tablet is not connected. Try reconnecting them.

Please make sure that the device you are trying to connect with have its Bluetooth turned on and discoverable. If you have problem connecting a Bluetooth device, try restarting your tablet. You can restart your device by pressing the power button until the device restarts.

The following are the Bluetooth Profiles supported by Amazon tablet.

- Advanced Audio Distribution Profile (A2DP)
- Audio/Video Remote Control Profile (AVRCP)
- Human Interface Device Profile (HID)
- Serial Port Profile (SPP)

Location Services

Enabling location service allows Map, Amazon and some apps to serve you content related services. More importantly, it enables Amazon to trace your Fire tablet in case of lost.

Note: You may have to activate location service in order to receive information and search the map.

To Activate Find Your Tablet/Location Services:

1. Swipe down from the top of the screen to open the quick actions menu, and then tap **Settings.**
2. Tap on **Device Options**.
3. Tap the switch next to **Find Your Tablet.**
4. If prompted, tap **Enable.**

Find My Device Feature

You can use this feature to locate your tablet if lost.

To find you lost tablet

1. Visit **www.amazon.com/mycd** and log in to your account
2. Go to **Your Device** tab located at the upper center of the screen (if you are browsing with a desktop)
3. Go to **Device Actions** tab to access action menu.
4. From this menu, you can perform the following actions:

1. **Deregister:** This option can be used to deregister your tablet.

2. **Remote Alarm:** This option can be used to turn on alarm so that the tablet can make sound, which may help in locating it. This alarm should last for two minutes.

3. **Find my Device:** This option can be used to access the last known location of your tablet.

4. **Remote Lock:** This will allow you to lock the tablet with a new password so as to prevent unwanted access. You can also include a message to display on the lock screen using this feature.

5. **Remote Factory Reset:** This feature allows you to reset your tablet to factory settings. Only choose this option if you are convinced that you may never find your tablet again. This is because you will no longer be able to track your tablet if you select this option. You may need a battery level of 30% to perform this action.

Note:

- To find your device with this option, you must turn on **Find My Device** (see page 100) feature before you misplaced the tablet.
- Your lost tablet must be on and connected to a network to allow Amazon to find your device. According to Amazon, if your lost tablet is off or not connected to a network, Amazon will keep trying to reach your tablet for three days.

Alternative way to find your device

1. Download and install **Lookout Security & Antivirus** from Amazon Appstore.
2. Launch the app and register your account. Then go to **missing device** tab in order to customize relevant settings.

This app can be used to find your missing tablet. It also protects your tablet from malwares and can be used to back up your data.

Entertainment

Using the Camera

Fire tablets (fifth generation) come with both rear-facing camera and front-facing cameras. With these cameras, you can capture a photo or record a video.

Note: The memory capacity of the picture taken may differ depending on the shooting scene and shooting conditions.

Hint: Both photos and videos can be backed up automatically on the cloud when on Wi-Fi.

To enable this feature, open the **Photos app** and swipe from the left edge of the screen. Then tap **Settings** and tap the switch next to **Photos and Videos** (under **Auto-save).**

Amazon allows you to save unlimited photo on the cloud.

> ➤ **To Capture a photo**

1. Open the application grid and select the **Camera.** If you are in a lock screen, swipe from the bottom right corner of the screen to access the camera app.

2. Aim the lens at the subject and make any necessary adjustments. By default, Fire tablet will focus the center of the screen unless a face is detected. To focus any part of the screen, tap that part of the screen.

3. Tap **front-facing/rear-facing icon** to switch between the rear-facing and front-facing camera.

4. To zoom in, place two fingers on the screen and spread them apart. Do the reverse to zoom out.

5. If available, tap the camera Flash icon to manage the flash settings. You can choose **On**, **Off** or **Auto**.

6. Tap on **shutter button** to take a photo. To capture many photos, press and hold the shutter button.

7. After taking photos, you may select the image viewer to view the photos.

> ➢ **To customize camera settings**

To use the lenticular setting

1. Repeat the step 1 above.

2. Tap on the setting icon and tap on the **Lenticular**

3. Aim the lens at the subject and make any necessary adjustments.

4. Tap on the **Shutter button** to take the shorts. Lenticular images are usually saved in form of animated .gif files.

To use Panorama setting

This feature allows you to capture picture with elongated field of view. For example you will find this feature important when trying to take the picture of a stadium or waterfall because of the large field of view. The panorama feature presents on Fire tablet can be used to create an extended horizontal or vertical image.

1. Open the application grid and select the **Camera**.

2. Tap on the setting icon and tap on the **Panorama**

3. Aim the lens at the subject and make any necessary adjustments.

4. Tap the **Shutter icon** and the move the tablet a little to get a full view of what you are capturing.

5. Your tablet automatically stitches the multiple images together to create an extended corresponding vertical or horizontal image.

Hint: To get a good quality picture when taking panoramic picture, it is advisable to avoid taking the picture of fast moving objects or moving your tablet very fast.

HDR

High Dynamic Range (HDR) allows you to take more detailed and better-looking pictures depending on when you use it. Sometimes, HDR is Ok and using it will allow you to get better-looking pictures but sometimes it may not be necessary to use it.

Recording a video

1. Open the application grid and select the **Camera.** If you are in a lock screen, swipe from the bottom right corner of the screen to access the camera app.

2. Aim the lens at the subject and make any necessary adjustments. By default, Amazon fire tablet will focus the center of the screen unless a face is detected. To focus any part of the screen, tap that part of the screen.

3. Tap on the **video button** to start recording

4. To zoom in while recording, place two fingers on the screen and spread them apart. To zoom out, move the two fingers closer together.

5. When done with the recording, tap the **video button** 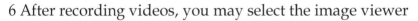 again.

6 After recording videos, you may select the image viewer

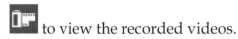 to view the recorded videos.

Hint: To capture pictures while recording a video, tap the

shutter icon

Note: If the feature is enabled, both the photos and the videos on your tablet are automatically backed up on amazon server when connected to Wi-Fi. Please go to the beginning of this chapter to learn how to enable automatic backup.

Editing Your Photos

You can use your tablet to edit photos.

1. Open the app grid and tap on **Photos**. Alternatively, you

may access your photos by tapping the **Image Viewer** located on your camera screen.

2. Tap on the photo you want to edit.

3. While viewing the photo, tap the photo to show the toolbar.

4. Then tap the **Edit icon.** Select the editing tool of your choice.

5. To delete a photo, tap the delete button.

Managing your photos

1. Open the app grid and tap on **Photos**.
2. Swipe from the left edge of the screen and select:
    a. **All** – Include all photos and personal videos stored on your device or in Cloud Drive.
    b. **Videos** - Include personal videos stored on your device or in Cloud Drive.
    c. **Camera Roll** – Include your recent photos and videos taken with your camera.
    d. **Cloud Drive** - Include photos and videos stored in Cloud Drive.
    e. **Device** - Include photos and videos downloaded to your Fire tablet, or photos and videos downloaded from the Internet or email attachments.
3. To add photos to device from another device or app, tap **Add Photos** and select a device or app from the list and then follow the onscreen instructions to complete the importing process.

Viewing your photos

1. Open the app grid and tap on **Photos**.
2. Tap a photo to view
3. Rotate your tablet vertically to enter the **portrait mode** and swipe from the right edge of the screen towards the middle to view a timeline of your photos in months or year.

4. Press and hold a photo to activate the selection tool in order to select multiple photos to share, delete or upload to the cloud.

5. To view your photos/videos in mosaic, rotate your tablet horizontally to enter **landscape mode**.

Using the Video Player

You can use Fire Tablet native video player to play videos that are present on your device.

Notes: The native video player on your tablet supports not all video formats. If you see that you can't access or watch a particular video, it may be that the file type of the video is not supported.

 ➢ **To access and play videos**

The videos you record with your tablet camera and those ones you transfer from your PC to your tablet will be under **My Videos** or **Photos**.

1. To access your videos, open the application grid and select **Photos** or **My Videos**. Search for the video you want to play and then tap on it.

2. Control playback with **virtual keys** (see the next page).

Media Player Virtual Keys

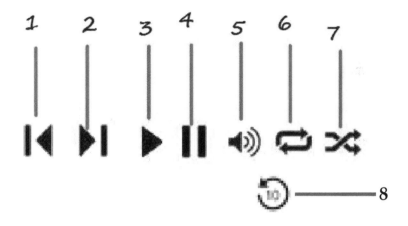

Number	Function
1.	Go to previous track
2.	Go to next track
3.	Play button
4.	Pause
5.	Volume button.
6.	Tap once to repeat all the media in the playlist. Tap twice to repeat the current song

	repeatedly.
7.	Shuffle all the media in an album or playlist.
8.	Jump back or forward in a title by a particular amount of time. This time is usually indicated at the center of the icon.

Settings

Settings menu give you the opportunity to customize your device as you like.

To access the settings menu

1. Swipe down from the top of the screen to open the quick access menu and then tap on **Settings.**
2. Alternatively, you can tap settings icon from the app grid.

The following are options under the settings tab:

Wireless

This option allows you to connect to Wi-Fi network and access the internet or other network devices. To use options under **Wireless,** please refer to page 95.

Storage

This option allows you to manage you storage.

To manage your device memory:

1. Swipe down from the top of the screen to open the quick actions menu, and then tap **Settings.**

2. Tap on **Storage** to view available memory.

3. Tap **Internal Storage** to view storage by content category. Tap a content category to see the file names and sizes. To delete an item, select the checkbox next to the item, and then tap **Remove**. Please note that Fire tablet will prevent you if you are trying to delete an essential item (i.e. those items necessary for the proper functioning of your device).

4. You can tap on **Archive Now** to see if any of your file qualifies for **1-Tap Archive** so as to free up space.

5. Tap on **View Contents** to view the storage space of contents on your device.

6. To view and manage the storage used by household profiles on your device (if you have created one), tap on a profile name.

Hint: Since contents in a child's profile also contribute to overall device storage, you may wish to manage your child's content. To do this, launch the child's profile from a lock screen and repeat steps 1 to 3 above.

In addition, you may remove a content from a child profile by activating the child profile. Then tap a content library, such as **Books**. Press and hold the downloaded item you want to remove, and then tap **Remove from Device**.

Managing SD Card Storage

Please refer to page 4 for more information on this.

Power

This option allows you to manage the power settings on your device.

To view your battery usage

1. Swipe down from the top of the screen to open the quick actions menu, and then tap **Settings.**
2. Tap on **Power** to view battery status.

Smart Suspend

Smart suspend is a feature that suspends unnecessary features like wireless when not in use. It helps conserve battery life. This feature can be set to manually or automatically manage your tablet's battery life. By default this feature is enabled. To disable this feature:

1. Repeat step 1 and 2 above
2. Tap the switch next to **Automatic Smart Suspend** or **Scheduled Smart Suspend** and set a time.

Display Settings:

Display settings affect battery life and you can manage it using this option. To manage your display settings:

1. Swipe down from the top of the screen to open the quick actions menu, and then tap **Settings**
2. Tap on **Power**.
3. Tap **Display Settings** and adjust necessary settings under this tab in order to conserve your battery life.

Hint: Choosing a lower time to sleep (e.g five minutes) and choosing lower screen brightness may help conserve the battery life. In addition, choosing not to rotate the screen may also help conserve battery life.

Wireless Settings

Wireless Settings affect battery life and you can manage it using this option. To manage your Wireless Settings:

1. Repeat the first two steps above.
2. Tap **Wireless Settings** and adjust the necessary settings to conserve your battery life.

Note: If you're really concerned about conserving battery life, as a rule, wireless should be off when not in use.

Apps & Games

This feature allows you to manage your applications and games settings.

To configure amazon application settings:
1. Swipe down from the top of the screen to open the quick actions menu, and then tap **Settings**
2. Tap on **Apps & Games**.
3. Then tap on **Amazon Application Settings.**

To manage applications on your device:
1. Repeat steps 1 and 2 above.
2. Tap on **Manage All Applications.**

3. Then tap on the particular application to you want to manage from the list of applications. *Notes:*

- You can use this option to force quit or uninstall an application. You can choose **force stop** if you notice that the app is not behaving properly. This will stop the app from carrying out any process on your tablet. To enable the app again, just launch the app. You may also consider uninstalling the app if you find out that you do not need the app again.

- You also have the option to **clear data** or **clear cache** of the app. When you choose **clear data**, all the stored information like settings of the app will be lost but the app will not be uninstalled. This implies that the next time you launch the app, you will be using it as if you are using it for the first time. When you choose **clear cache**, the cache memory is cleared. Cache is a set of data stored on a computer memory so that you can get a faster response when using an item.

Hint: You can turn on the installation from platform other than Amazon, please go to section on **Security** (see page 125) to learn more.

Collect App Usage Data

Enable this option if you want Amazon appstore to collect usage data of your downloaded apps.

Display

This option allows you control those aspects of your tablet that has to do with display

To adjust your screen brightness

- Please refer to page 18.

To turn off automatic screen rotation

- Please refer to page 9.

To Change the Time to Sleep

You can set your tablet to sleep after a specified time. To effect this, tap on the **Display Sleep** located under **Display** tab, and then set the time of your choice.

To configure font size

Tap on the **Font Size** located under **Display** tab, and then choose a font size.

Note: Please note that Display Mirroring is not supported on All-New Fire HD 8 (6th Generation).

Device Options

Device settings give you the opportunity to manage many settings associated with your tablet.

To change the name of your device:

1. Swipe down from the top of the screen to open the quick actions menu, and then tap **Settings**
2. Tap on **Device Options**.

3. Tap on **Change Your Device Name**

To change the date and time

- Please refer to page 16.

Find Your Tablet

Please refer to page 101 to learn more about how to find your device when lost.

To enable auto backups

It is advisable to back up your tablet to be on a safer side in case of damage or loss. Data from settings, notes, silk browser bookmarks, and more are backed up.

Note that purchased products such as apps, books, video, and audios are automatically back up in Amazon cloud.

1. Swipe down from the top of the screen to open the quick actions menu, and then tap **Settings**
2. Tap on **Device Options**.
3. Tap on **Backup & Restore.**
4. Tap the switch next to **Device Backup**.
5. Your tablet will automatically back up once daily when connected to Wi-Fi and it is in sleep mode.

Note: If you have backed up your tablet, you will have the opportunity to access your files when you set up a new tablet.

To install system updates

1. Repeat steps 1 and 2 above

2. Tap on the **System Updates**

3. Tap on **Install system updates** to install updates

Please note that installing system updates may sometime make you lose access to some of tweaks you have done to your device.

To carry out factory reset:

1. Swipe down from the top of the screen to open the quick actions menu, and then tap **Settings**

2. Tap on **Device Options**.

3. Tap on **Reset to Factory Defaults**

4. Tap on **Reset**.

When you perform factory reset on your device, you will still be able to access your items that are backed up in the cloud. Generally, it is recommended you backup (see page 120) your device before you perform a factory reset.

To get information about your fire tablet

1. Repeat steps 1 and 2 above

2. Then tap on **Device model**

3. The serial number of your device is shown under **Serial Number** tab.

My Accounts

This option allows you to manage your account with Amazon and social network accounts.

1. Swipe down from the top of the screen to open the quick actions menu, and then tap **Settings**
2. Tap on the **My Accounts** tab
3. Select any of the following options in the list:

A. Deregister your tablet: This option allows you to remove the account registered with your tablet and enter another one. You may find this option useful if you find out that a wrong account is linked to your tablet or you wish to change the account to a different one.

B. Manage your Amazon account settings: This option gives the opportunity to manage your Amazon account and customize it. In addition, under this setting, you can choose which payment method to use when you purchase a product from Amazon.

C. Manage your social network: This feature gives you the option of customizing your social network accounts. You will able to add/manage social network account under this feature.

To link Facebook and Twitter

1. From **Settings,** tap **My Accounts,** and then tap **Social Networks.**

2. Then tap **Connect Your Twitter Account**, **Connect Your Facebook Account**, or **Goodreads**

3. Enter the account information for your social network, and then tap **Connect**.

4. Note that you can unlink your social account at any time.

Profiles & Family Library

Use these settings to manage your child's profiles and family library. Please go to sections on **household profiles** (see page 66) and **Amazon FreeTime** (see page 60) to learn more.

Parental Controls

Parental controls

This feature allows you to set up security on some features present on your fire tablet.

To set up parental controls

1. Swipe down from the top of the screen to open the quick actions menu, and then tap **Settings.**
2. Tap on **Parental Controls**.
3. Then tap the switch next to **Parental controls**
4. Enter a password of your choice and tap **Finish.**
5. To **disable parental controls** at any time, tap the switch again.
6. Using this feature, you can restrict one or more of the following features:

i. Web browser

ii. Camera

iii. Social Networks

iv. Email and Calendar

v. The ability to play videos on Amazon Instant Video

vi. Wireless and mobile network connectivity

vii. Location-Based Services

viii. The ability to purchase content on your device

ix. Specific content types like books

From the parental controls menu, you can also manage your child's profile, to do this, tap on the child's profile. You will see a padlock icon at the top of the screen when parental controls are active on your device.

Security

To Allow non-Amazon app installation

Allowing the installation applications from third parties or from stores other than Amazon Appstore is very important when you want to get around the restriction posed by Amazon limited Appstore. By enabling this feature, you will be able to install many apps from stores other than Amazon.

1. Swipe down from the top of the screen to open the quick actions menu, and then tap **Settings**
2. Tap on **Security**
3. Tap the switch next to **Apps from Unknown Sources**.

Note: I will advise that for security reason you turn this feature off whenever you are not using it, only turn it on when you want to install third parties app from a source other than Amazon.

Lock Screen

Please refer to page 18.

Credential Storage

This allows you to access all stored digital certificates.

Device Administrators

This option allows you view which applications are authorized as device administrators for your Fire tablet.

Sounds & Notifications

This feature allows you to configure your sound and notification settings. Please refer to page 17 learn more.

Keyboard & Language

Use this option to control the keyboard and language settings on your device.

Manage keyboard and Language

Please refer to the preceding section on **keyboard & language** (page 15) to learn more.

Text-to-Speech

Please refer to page 53 to learn more.

Current Keyboard

This tab displays the current keyboard you are using on your device.

Show/Hide Keyboards

This tab allows you to tell your device which keyboard can be set as default.

Sync Device

Use this feature to sync your device so that it can receive contents from the cloud and receive new software updates.

Help

Use this option to get help information on your device and also contact Amazon technical support.

Accessibility

This option allows you to manage accessibility feature on your device, for more information on this, please refer to preceding chapter on **Accessibility** (page 47).

Legal & Compliance

This feature gives you information on privacy policies, terms of use, and legal notices for your device.

What You Must Know About Your Fire Tablet

Removing Special Offers Banner

If you purchased a Special Offers Fire Tablet you will be charged a one-time payment to unsubscribe from the service.

To unsubscribe from Special Offers:

1. Launch www.amazon.com/mycd.
2. Click on **Your Device** tab
3. Click on your device name to display more options.
4. Next to **Special Offers,** click **Edit,** and then follow the onscreen instructions to unsubscribe from Special Offers.

How to take screenshot on your device

Another task you can perform on your device is taking a screenshot. To take a screenshot with your device, please follow the instructions below:

1. Navigate to the required page (the page you want to take its screenshot).
2. Place one finger on the volume down button and the other finger on the power button and press these two buttons simultaneously.
3. To locate your screenshots, from the App Grid on the Home screen, tap **Photos**, and then swipe from the left edge of the screen and tap **All/Screenshot**.

How To Find Your Tablet When lost

As a human being, it is not impossible that you may misplace your tablet. If someone else (a thief) has not taken custody of it, there are steps to follow in order to find it. These steps have been discussed at length on page 101-103; please refer to it for details.

Amazon Limited App – You have little To Worry About

All-New Fire HD 8 Tablet (6th Generation, 2016 Edition) came with Fire OS. This OS is a forked version of Android OS, i.e. Fire OS was built by making some changes to Android OS. Thus, many applications that normally work on Android OS will work on Fire OS.

However, considering the fact that Fire OS is not entirely similar to Android OS, you may still have some apps that are working on Android OS but will refuse to work on Fire OS. Anyway, many apps that work on Android OS will also work on Fire OS and you should be able to install many apps present on Google Play but not on Amazon Appstore by sideloading these apps on your tablet.

How to sideload an app on Amazon Fire Tablet

A. The first thing to do when sideloading an app is to change your settings so that you tablet can allow the installation of non-Amazon app. You can follow the steps below:

1. Swipe down from the top of the screen to open the quick actions menu, and then tap **Settings**
2. Tap on **Security**

3. Tap the switch next to **Apps from Unknown Sources**.

Note: I will advise that for security reason you turn this feature off whenever you are not using it, only turn it on when you want to install third parties app from a source other than Amazon.

B. Download and install this **ES File Explorer** from Amazon Appstore. This app will enable you to locate any application file you download from the internet.

C. Download the Apk of the app you want to sideload. To do this:

1. Go to play.google.com from your silk browser
2. Search for the app of your choice in the store
3. Then copy the address of the application from the address of bar of your silk browser
4. Type apps.evozi.com/apk-downloader into the silk browser and launch it
5. Then paste the address you copied in step 3 into the address bar found on the webpage.
6. Click on **Generate Download Link**
7. Then tap on **Click here to Download...**
8. If prompted to select an application to complete the downloading process, select Silk browser and follow onscreen instructions to complete the download.

D. Open the ES File Explorer App, and locate **Download** in the drop down menu. This will show you the files you have downloaded on your tablet. Tap on the file of the app you want to install and then tap on install.

E. When you are done installing the app, go the app grid and look for the app you have just installed. With this method, you should be able to install as many as possible apps.

Alternatively, you may first download the app apk to your PC, and then transfer it to your tablet using the USB cable.

To learn how to sideload Google Play store please refer to the **bonus chapter** on page 146.

Top App to Consider For Sideloading

There are many app to consider for sideloading depending on nature of your work or what you use your tablet to do most. The first app I will advise you to sideload is 1Mobile Market. This is an online application store for android devices. If you have a store like this on your tablet you may not really need to download apk of individual applications again. This is because all you need to do is to open 1Mobile Market app, search for apps of your choice, and then install it. As simple as ABC. However, you will have to allow the installation of non Amazon apps before you can install apps from 1Mobile Market.

Note: Because of risk of exposing yourself to malwares, I will advise that you have antivirus like Lookout Antivirus or Mobile Security & Antivirus on your tablet.

How to Access Google Drive And Other Cloud Drives Easily

There is a cool way to access Google drive and other cloud drives without having to sideload their apps. You can follow the steps below to get this done.

1. Download **ES File Explorer** from Amazon Appstore and install it (you can skip this step if you have already done so).
2. Open the app and tap on **Network** and then tap on **Cloud**.
3. Tap on add icon (+ icon) located at the lower part of the screen to add any of DropBox, OneDrive, Gdrive, SugarSync etc.
4. Follow the onscreen instruction to complete the setup.

Solution to Non-Responding Apps

Sometimes an app may start misbehaving and may even refuse to close. The first thing you can do is to tap on the task-switcher button (the button besides the home button) to see all recently opened apps or items. Locate this particular app, and tap on **X** icon to close it.

Try launching the app again. If it is still misbehaving then you may follow these steps:

4. Swipe down from the top of the screen to open the quick actions menu, and then tap **Settings**

5. Tap on **Apps & Games**.

6. Then tap on **Manage All Applications**

7. Then tap on the misbehaving application from the list of applications

8. Select **force stop**. This will stop the app from carrying out any process on your tablet. To enable the app again, just launch the app.

You also have the option to clear data, or clear cache of the app. When you choose clear data, all the stored information like settings of the app will be lost but the app will not be uninstalled. This means that the next time you launch the app, you will be using it as if you are using it for the first time. When you choose clear cache, the cache memory is cleared. Cache is a set of data stored on a computer memory so that future requests for data can be served faster.

How To conserve Fire Tablet' s Battery Life

You may notice that you have to charge Fire tablet twice a day in order to keep your tablet on. There are steps to follow to ensure that your tablet serves you tryout the day with just a single charge.

1. **Reduce the screen brightness:** I have realized over time that screen brightness consumes a lot of energy. There is usually a substantial difference between using a tablet with a maximum brightness and using it with a moderate brightness. As a rule, don't use your tablet with a maximum brightness unless you can't see what is on the screen clearly, for example, if you are outdoor, and please make sure you reduce it immediately when it is no more needed.

2. **Shorten the Screen timeout:** If you really want to save your battery you must try to shorten the **screen timeout** (see page 119). Reducing how long your tablet will stay lit up after you finish interacting with it will really help you to save battery.

3. **Turn off Wi-Fi and Bluetooth:** When you are not using Wi-Fi or Bluetooth please always remember to put them off. These features really suck energy and they are better off when not in use.

4. **Reduce number of notifications:** There are two benefits of doing this, the first is that there will be less distractions and the second benefit is that notification sucks energy. Limit yourself to those notifications that are important to your life. To learn how to disable notifications for individual app, please see page 17.

5. **Close all unnecessary apps:** The truth is that any app you open is using out of the limited battery energy. It is important to close any app you are not using from time to time. To access all apps currently running on your tablet, tap on the task-switcher button ▪ the button besides the home button). To close any of the opened apps, tap on **X** icon.

6. **Use a correct charger:** Using wrong charger can endanger the health of your tablet/battery, and it is better to avoid such practice.

7. **Consider switching off your tablet:** If you are not going to use your tablet for an extended period, you may consider switching off your tablet.

8. **Use headphones:** Using the headphones is another cool way to save your battery. Extended use of audio speakers of your tablet may drain your battery faster.

How to read EPUB on your device

You can read EPUB books using overdrive app. This is particularly cool since some books are in EPUB format and not in Kindle format.

If books through your local library system are not available on Kindle, they are usually in an EPUB format. This app makes getting and reading books in this format easy.

To download and install Overdrive app, To download and install Overdrive app, please go to **http://pharmibrahim.blogspot.com/2015/10/blog-post_24.html**.

Download this app and follow the onscreen instructions to set it up.

How to send personal document to your fire tablet or any Kindle device

One way to send personal documents to your device is through USB which I have already discussed on page 95. However, I will like to discuss another way to send personal document to your Fire tablet. This is through the use of **Send-to-Kindle E-mail.**

Send-to-Kindle E-mail is a unique address that is assigned to you when you register your compatible Fire tablet, Kindle e-reader or supported Kindle reading app.

The files supported on Send-to-Kindle include DOC, DOCX, HTML, PDF, TXT, GIF, RTF, JPEG, PNG, BMP, PRC, and MOBI. You can send any of your documents in the format mentioned above to your Kindle.

To view your Send-to-Kindle E-mail:

1. Launch https://www.amazon.com/mycd from your browser
2. Tap on **Settings** tab and scroll down to **Personal Document Settings**.
3. Locate the **Send-to-Kindle E-mail address** corresponding to the name of your device**.**

4. To edit your **Send-to-Kindle E-mail,** tap **Edit** next to the email you want to change.

Sending documents to your Send-to-Kindle E-mail address

To send a document to your Kindle device or app, simply attach it to an e-mail addressed to your Send-to-Kindle e-mail.

Notes:

- It is not necessary to include a subject in the email.
- Total size of the documents you want to send should not be more than 50 MB and your email should not contain more than 25 attachments in order to avoid running into any problem.
- Amazon makes it possible to be able to add notes, highlights, and bookmarks to your personal documents. In addition, your notes, highlights and bookmarks are synchronized across devices along with the last page read via Whispersync technology. Note that this synchronization feature is only available for personal documents archived in Kindle format. Interestingly, some documents formats are supported by the Amazon conversion service, but charges may apply.

Adding/Deleting an Approved Email Address

Documents can only be sent to your Kindle device from e-mail accounts that you have been added to Approved Personal Document E-mail List.

To add/delete an approved e-mail address:

1. Launch www.amazon.com/mycd
2. Click on **Settings** tab and scroll down to **Personal Document Settings**.
3. Under **Approved Personal Document List**, click on **Add a new approved e-mail address**.
4. Enter the desired e-mail address and click **Add Address**.
5. To remove an approved e-mail address, click on **Delete** next to the address you wish to remove.

Extras

Getting an antivirus for your tablet -- is it necessary?

Many people may not really take the issue of antivirus serious because they think that virus software target PC much more than tablets. The truth is that things are changing every now and then. The best thing you can do is to always keep a guard. There are many reputable free antiviruses on Amazon Appstore. My favorite antiviruses are **AVG, Lookout and Mobile Security and Antivirus**. You may visit this webpage **http://pharmibrahim.blogspot.com/2015/10/blog-post_24.html** to download any of these apps.

Safety Precautions When Using Fire Tablet on Wi-Fi

With many free Wi-Fi hotspots, it is likely that you are going to find yourself using Wi-Fi more on your tablet. There are few things to keep in mind when using Wi-Fi.

1. Confirm the Network Name

Hackers sometimes set up a fake Wi-Fi network in order to tap into the information of unwitting public users. To avoid this, make sure you are sure of the name of the network you are connecting to. You may ask any trusted individual around you if you doubt the name of a network.

2. Connect To Secure Site

Whenever you are sending sensitive information always make sure that the site is a secure website. You can know whether a website is a secured site or not by checking whether the URL address of the website starts with **HTTPS.** If it starts with https, then it should be a secure site.

3. Run an Antivirus Software

As earlier mentioned, using an antivirus is very crucial in today's world. You may consider installing a genuine antivirus. My recommended antivirus can be found on **http://pharmibrahim.blogspot.com/2015/10/blog-post_24.html**

4. Get a Virtual Private Network (VPN)

It is highly important you use a virtual private network when using a public network. There are both free and paid VPN providers. My favorite is Hotspot Shield VPN. It is available on Amazon Appstore. They offer both free and paid version. You may also check out other VPN apps to pick the best.

5. Avoid Automatic Connection

Make sure your Wi-Fi is off when not using it to avoid your tablet automatically connecting to an open network. Turning your Wi-Fi off when not using it will also save your battery energy.

I am Having a Dwindling Love for my Fire Tablet; What Should I do?

It is possible that after buying All-New Fire HD 8 Tablet (6th Generation, 2016 Edition), you realize that it performs below your expectation. It is likely that you dislike your tablet because of its hardware or software issue. Generally, the hardware has to do with the design, the tablet make up, the weight of the tablet etc. while the software has to do with OS and applications.

If your love for All-New Fire HD 8 Tablet (6th Generation, 2016 Edition) is reducing because of the software; there is a way out. Although Amazon Appstore may not be robust enough, there are ways to sideload many great apps on your device. Sidelaoding great apps should transform your experience with Fire tablet. It is likely that with the right apps, you may have little or no problem with your device. You can check page 131 to learn more about sideloading an app.

If your love for Fire tablet is reducing because of the hardware then it is either you learn how to live with it (you may have to force yourself to love it) or you sell it.

How to Sideload Google Play Store on Fire Tablet

You can follow the steps below to sideload Google Play.

You will need ES File Explorer to complete this process and since I have mentioned this app several times, I will assume that you have already installed it, so I will not talk about its installation again.

1. Visit this URL address
   **https://onedrive.live.com/?id=DE44F9BE97C25F7F%211389&ci
   d=DE44F9BE97C25F7F**
   If you have problem typing this URL address into your web browser then go to this webpage
   http://pharmibrahim.blogspot.com/2015/10/google-apk.html
   (You will see a link to download the apks when you get there).
2. Download the four folders contained in the download link
3. Open **ES File Explorer** and locate the download folder
4. Then tap on the apk files you have downloaded to install them in this order:
   i. Google Account Manager
   ii. Google Play Services

iii. Google Services Framework

iv. Google Play Store

Notes:

- The order of installation of the various Google apks has been found to be important, hence please make sure that you follow the correct order of installation so as to make sure you get the desired result.

- You may need to turn off Amazon store auto update feature in order to preempt any errors.

- If you have not changed your settings to allow the installation of non Amazon apps, then you will need to do so before you can install the four folders above. Please refer to page 125 to know how to change your settings.

- I cannot guarantee that this approach will continue to work, and I will advise that you also install alternative apps stores like 1Mobile Market, and Mobogenie.

- Please if this approach does not work for you, try contacting me @ **pharmibrahimguides@gmail.com**

Troubleshooting

If the touch screen responds slowly or improperly or your tablet is not responding, try the following:

- Remove any protective covers (screen protector) from the touch screen.
- Ensure that your hands are clean and dry when tapping.
- Press the power button once to lock the screen and press it again to unlock the screen and enter a PIN/password if required.
- Press and hold the **Power** button until your device restarts automatically.

Your Tablet Doesn't Charge

- Make sure you are using Amazon charger to charge your tablet.
- If the Fire tablet does not indicate that it is charging, unplug the power adapter and then restart your device.
- Make sure you are using the micro-USB cable that came with the Fire tablet or anyone that has similar specs.

Forgot Lock Screen Password or PIN

1. Go to **www.amazon.com/mycd**
2. Click on **Your Devices**
3. Then select your Fire tablet from the list of devices registered to your account.

4. Open the **Device Actions** drop-down menu and select **Remote lock.**

5. Enter and then confirm a new password or PIN, and then select **lock Device.**

6. Tap **Unlock** Device on your tablet and then enter the new password or PIN you just created and tap **OK.**

Alternatively:

1. From the lock screen on your device, enter the wrong password/PIN five times.

2. After the fifth incorrect attempt, a notification will appear with options.

3. Select **Reset Your PIN** from these options.

4. Enter your Amazon account password, and tap **Continue.**

5. Enter your new PIN/Password, and then tap **Finish.**

Your device is hot to the touch

When you use applications that require more power or use applications on your device for an extended period of time, your tablet may be a bit hot to touch. This is normal and it should not affect performance. You may just allow your tablet to rest for some time or close some applications.

Your tablet is not responding to touch

Make sure you have not accidentally turned On **VoiceView** (see page 47). If you have not, then try restarting your device.

Your tablet freezes or has fatal error

If your tablet freezes or it is unresponsive, press and hold the power button until your device restarts automatically.

Tablet does not connect Wi-Fi

Make sure you don't have limited network connectivity in that area. If your network is good and you still cannot connect, you may perform any of these actions:

- Make sure you Airplane Mode is off.
- Try restarting the Wi-Fi settings.
- Move closer to your router and scan for the available networks. If the network still does not shows up, you may add the network manually.
- Restart your router and modem. Unplug the modem and router for few minutes and plug the modem in and then the router.
- Try restarting you tablet.

Another Bluetooth device is not located

- Ensure Bluetooth feature is activated on your tablet and the device you want to connect to.
- Ensure that your tablet and the other Bluetooth device are within the maximum Bluetooth range.
- Ensure that the device you are trying to connect with is having a supported Bluetooth profile. Please refer to page 100 to find the list of supported Bluetooth profiles.

A connection is not established when you connect your tablet to a PC

- Ensure that the USB cable you are using is compatible with your device.

- Ensure that you have the proper drivers installed and updated on your PC.

Purchased content not showing

- Verify that your tablet is registered to the correct Amazon account. To confirm your registration, go to **my account** under settings tab and check the registered name. If you see a wrong account, tap **Deregister** and then register a new account.

Safety precautions

A. To prevent electric shock, fire, and explosion

1. Do not use damaged power cords or plugs, or loose electrical sockets.
2. Do not touch the power cord with a wet hand.
3. Do not bend or damage the power cord.
4. Do not short-circuit the charger.
5. Do not use your tablet during thunderstorm.
6. Do not dispose your tablet by putting it in fire.

B. Follow all safety warnings and regulations when using your device in restricted areas.

C. Comply with all safety warnings and regulations regarding mobile device usage while operating a vehicle.

D. Proper care and use of your tablet

1. Keep your tablet dry. Your tablet is not water resistant.
2. Do not use or store your tablet in hot or cold areas. It is recommended to use your device at temperature from 5^0C to 35^0C.
3. Do not put your tablet near magnetic fields.
4. Do not use camera flash close to eyes of people or pets because it can cause temporary loss of vision or damage the eyes.

5. When cleaning your tablet, do not use chemicals or detergents. You may use small towel

6. Keep your tablet away from small children because they may mistakenly damage it. It may look like a toy to them.

Bonus Chapter

Alexa

Amazon has finally decided to include its virtual assistant on Fire tablets. This feature will transform the way you use Fire HD 8.

Alexa is a trained virtual assistant that has been built to answer questions. This section of the guide will show you how to manage Alexa like a pro and how to ask questions and give commands that Alexa will understand.

Disabling/Enabling Alexa

You can disable or enable Alexa by following the steps below:

4. Swipe down from the top of the screen to open the quick actions menu, and then tap **Settings**
5. Tap on **Device Options**.
6. Tap the switch next to **Alexa**.

Please note that Alexa will be disabled if you have **Parental Controls** (see page 123-124) turned on for your tablet. To use Alexa, you may have to disable Parental Controls. In addition, Alexa does not work within a child profile on your Fire tablet.

Speaking to Alexa

One of the ways you will interact with Alexa is by saying your questions. There are few things to know when talking to Alexa so as to get the best experience.

To get Alexa into action, you will need to get its attention. To do that, please follow the steps below:

1. Press and hold the Home button (the middle button at the lower part of the tablet) until you see a blue line at the bottom of the screen (you may also hear a tone).

2. Then speak your question to it. It will then give you an answer. If you want to ask another question, press and hold the Home button again.

Many times, Alexa will also display a card containing an answer in addition to the voice feedback. To dismiss this card, tap outside the card.

Notes:

- Please note that you may not be able to activate Alexa with a voice alone.
- In addition, because Alexa on your Fire tablet is not voice activated, you don't need to say Alexa (like you do when using Amazon Echo) whenever you are making request. All

you need to do when making a request is to press and hold the Home button and then make your request.

Using Alexa to open Apps or Programs

One of those things you will want to use Alexa to do is access your apps. You can quickly open an app by pressing and holding the Home button and then saying **Open** followed by the app's name. For example, to open calculator, say **Open calculator**.

Using Alexa with Different Types of Skills

You can give a new set of skills to Alexa using the Alexa app. So what is a skill? A skill is a special action performed by Alexa when it is connected to another device, app, website or item. For example, you can give Alexa some extra mathematical skills by connecting it to a third party app called **Math Puzzle.** In addition, you can give Alexa some flight information capabilities by connecting it to a third party app called **KAYAK.** Furthermore, you can give Alexa some smart control capabilities by connecting it to a skill called **SmartThings**.

In a nutshell, connecting a skill to Alexa transforms the way you use this voice assistant. It lets you do what you can't do with Alexa alone. In this section of the guide, you will be learning the basic steps to follow to connect a new skill to Alexa.

To add a skill to Alexa:

1. Open Alexa app and tap on the menu icon located at the top left corner of the screen.
2. Tap on **Skills**
3. Tap on **Categories** and choose a category and then a skill. Alternative, tap the Search bar located at the top of the screen and enter a search phrase.
4. Tap a skill and follow the onscreen instructions to link this skill to Alexa. Please note that you may be required to enter some account information to link a skill.
5. You are now ready to use the new skill.

Hints: To link a smart home device, just follow the steps 1 to 3 above and tap on **Smart Home** category. Then choose a skill and follow the prompts to enable this skill.

Do you want to use Alexa in a special way? Then add nice Skills to it. You can know how to use a particular Skill by reading the information on the details page of the Skill.

Connecting Your Smart Devices to Alexa

You can link many smart home devices by following the steps mentioned on page 156. However, not all smart home devices can be linked by following these steps. Some devices simply require you to have Alexa search for them on your W-Fi network and connect with them. To link those devices that don't require a skill:

1. Open Alexa app and tap on the menu icon ☰ located at the top left corner of the screen.
2. Tap on **Smart Home.**
3. Scroll down to **Your Devices** and tap on **Discover Devices.**
4. Alexa app will then begin scanning your network for any connected smart home devices. In the case of the Philips Hue system, any application or device (including Alexa app) that wants access to the Hue bridge requires you tap the physical button on the Hue bridge in order to authorize it. But other smart home products (like Belkin WeMo devices) may not require any physical tapping. So if you are using a Philips Hue system, make sure you tap the physical button on the Hue bridge before you tap the **Discover Devices** button on the Alexa app.
5. Then you will see the list of all discovered devices on the Alexa app. Tap **Forget** next to a device's name to prevent Alexa from controlling the device or to remove the device. Please note that if a device does not appear under the

discovered devices list, it may be that you will need to install the skill for the device instead. To install a skill for a smart home device, please go to page 156.

6. You are now ready to use your smart home devices with Alexa. But before you do that there is one more important thing to do and that is grouping your devices.

Tip: If after following the steps mentioned in this guide Alexa can't still discover your device, check the companion app for your smart home device to ensure that it's on the same Wi-Fi network as your Alexa app.

In addition, please note that if you turn off or unplug your smart home device and then turn it back on, it may take some time before Alexa app can rediscover the device.

Grouping Your Smart Home Devices

Grouping your smart home devices allow you to control them smartly. For example, you can create a group and name it **bedroom light** so that Alexa can access them whenever you make a command and you include bedroom light in the command. Please note that Alexa may not recognize any group you have created on your smart home device and you may need to create new groups using Alexa app.

To create a group:

1. Open Alexa app and tap on the menu icon located at the top left corner of the screen.
2. Tap on **Smart Home**
3. Under **Group,** tap **Create Group.**
4. Enter the group name in the field provided. Give your group a recognizable name for Alexa to identify. For example, you may use the name **Living Room light** to denote the light bulbs in your living room
5. Select the smart home device(s) you want to add to the group, and then select **Add/Save.**

To edit/manage a group:

1. Open Alexa app and tap on the menu icon located at the top left corner of the screen.
2. Tap on **Smart Home**
3. Under **Groups**, select your smart home group.
4. Make the necessary changes by tapping the required field.
5. To add or remove smart home devices, select the checkboxes next to each device.
6. To delete a group, tap **Delete.**

Using Alexa with Smart Home Devices

You can use Alexa to control your smart home devices. This is particularly interesting; imagine telling Alexa to turn on/off the light with just a voice command.

I will assume that you have already connected you smart home devices to your Alexa using the instructions provided on page 158.

After connecting your smart home device to Alexa, press and hold the Home button until you see a blue line or hear a sound and then then try any of these example commands:

- Turn on/off (smart home device/group name). For example, you may say **Turn off bedroom light**.

- Brighten/dim (smart home device/group name). For example, you may say **Brighten my living room light.** You may also say **Set my living room light to maximum**.

- Set (smart home device/group name) temperature to (lower/higher) degrees. For example, you may say **Set Samsung thermostat to 20 degrees.**

- Set (smart home device/group name) to "x". For example, you may say **Set Living room fan to 5.**

Note: As I have said before, you will need to connect your smart home devices to Alexa before you can use Alexa to control these devices. To learn how to connect Alexa to your smart device, please go to page 158.

Using Alexa with Your Calendar

One of the fantastic features that Alexa can do for you is making an appointment.

With just few commands you can get Alexa to put an event or appointment into your calendar. But before you can populate your calendar with events, you will need to first link your calendar to your Alexa app. To do this:

Please note that you may need to setup a Google calendar at **https://calendar.google.com** (if you don't already have one) before you can start adding events. To do this:

1. Open Alexa app and tap on the menu icon located at the top left corner of the screen.
2. Tap on **Settings**
3. Tap on **Calendar** and select **Google Calendar**
4. Select **Link Google Calendar account** and follow the prompts.
5. To unlink your calendar at a future time, tap **Unlink Google Calendar account.**

After linking your Google Calendar to Alexa, tap and hold the Home button until you see a blue line or hear a sound. Then say things like:

- **What is on my calendar tomorrow?**
- **Add an event to my calendar.**
- **How does my calendar look like today**?
- **Add meeting with Clinton to my calendar for Friday at 6 a.m.**
- **Add an appointment with Steve for Monday at 1 p.m.**

Please note that you can also say all the examples given above in another ways, the most important thing is to get Alexa to understand what you are saying.

Using Alexa with Your Shopping List and To-do List

There are probably many things going through your mind and it will be quite interesting if you can get a personal assistant to assist in putting it down inside a list. Fortunately, Alexa can help you in this regard.

To add an item to your to-do list or shopping list, tap and hold the Home button until you see a blue line or hear a sound. Then say things like:

- **Add 'go to my in-law house' to my to-do list**
- **Add (item) to my shopping list**
- **What's on my shopping list**
- **What's on my to-do list?**

Tip: You can manage your shopping or to-do list using Alexa app :

1. Open Alexa app and tap on the menu icon located at the top left corner of the screen.

2. Tap on **Shopping & To-do Lists**.

3. Select either list.

4. To add a new item to the list, tap the plus icon "+"

5. To delete an item from a list, tap the **V** icon next to the list you want to delete and tap **Delete item**. Alternatively, mark the checkbox next to an item and select **Delete.**

In addition, you can print your list if you are accessing Alexa app from a computer, to access Alexa app from a computer, go to http://alexa.amazon.com. Then in the left navigation menu click **Shopping & To-do Lists.** Choose either list. Then select **Print**.

Furthermore, you can link a third-party To-Do lists so that Alexa can make your Shopping List and To-do List available in third-party services. To do this:

1. Open Alexa app and tap on the menu icon located at the top left corner of the screen.

2. Tap on **Settings**.

3. Tap **Lists**.

4. Tap **Link** to the right of either Any.do or Todoist.

5. Enter your login information for the third-party service or create a new account and then follow the onscreen instructions to complete the linking process.

Using Alexa with Alarm

You can also set an alarm using this personal assistant. To do this, tap and hold the Home button until you see a blue line or hear a sound. Then try these example commands:

- **Set an alarm for 1 p.m. tomorrow**
- **Set an alarm for 30 minutes from now.**

Tip: To stop the alarm when it is sounding, press and hold the Home button and say **Stop the alarm**. You may also say **Snooze the alarm.** This will snooze the alarm for a particular period of time.

To set a repeating alarm, tap and hold the Home button until you see a blue line or hear a sound. Then say:

- **Set an everyday alarm for 7 a.m.**

To know the status of your alarm, tap and hold the Home button until you see a blue line or hear a sound. Then say things like:

- **What time is my alarm set for?**
- **What alarms do I have for Monday?**

To edit/delete an alarm use the Alexa app. To do this:

- Open Alexa app and tap on the menu icon located at the top left corner of the screen.
- Tap on **Timers & Alarms.**
- Choose your device from the drop-down menu.
- Select the **Alarms** tab.
- Choose the alarm you want to delete, and then select **Delete alarm**.

Tip: You may cancel an alarm with your voice. This will stop the alarm but may not delete it. For example if you have any alarm set for 8 p.m. on Friday, tap and hold the Home button until you see a blue line or hear a sound then say **Cancel my alarm for 8 p.m. on Friday.** This will cancel this particular alarm.

To change your alarm volume/sound:

1. Open Alexa app and tap on the menu icon located at the top left corner of the screen.

2. Tap on **Settings**

3. Select your device.

4. Tap **Sounds.**

5. To control the alarm volume, tap and drag the volume bar for **Alarm and Timer Volume**.

6. To change your alarm sound, select **Alarm Default Sounds**, and then pick a new sound.

7. To change the sound for a particular alarm, select the alarm you want to edit. Select **Alarm Sound**, and then pick a new sound.

Using Alexa with Timer

You can set a timer using this personal assistant. To do this, tap and hold the Home button until you see a blue line or hear a sound. Then try these example commands:

- **Set a timer for 30 minutes.**
- **Set the timer for 3 p.m.**

To stop the timer when it is sounding, tap and hold the Home button until you see a blue line or hear a sound, then say **Stop the timer**.

To know the status of your timer, tap and hold the Home button until you see a blue line or hear a sound, then say things like:

- **How much time is left on my timer?**

Tip: To dismiss a timer when it is sounding, tap the back button located at the bottom of the screen.

To edit/delete a timer:

1. Open Alexa app ![amazon alexa] and tap on the menu icon ![menu] located at the top left corner of the screen.
2. Tap on **Timers & Alarms.**
3. Choose your device from the drop-down menu.
4. Select the **Timers** tab.
5. Select **Edit** next to the timer you want to stop, and then tap **Cancel**.

You can also use your voice to delete an upcoming timer, tap and hold the Home button until you see a blue line or hear a sound and then say **Cancel the timer for (amount of time).**

To change your timer volume:

1. Open Alexa app and tap on the menu icon ![menu] located at the top left corner of the screen.
2. Tap on **Settings**

3. Select your device.

4. Tap **Sounds.**

5. Tap and drag the volume bar next to **Alarm and Timer Volume**.

Using Alexa with Clock

You can ask Alexa what your local time is. In addition, it can also tell you the time in a specific place. To do this, tap and hold the Home button until you see a blue line or hear a sound, then try these example commands:

- **What is the time?**
- **What is the time in New York?**

Using Alexa to Get Flight Information

You can also use this personal assistant to get information about a flight. This is a smarter way to know when a particular airplane will take off. To do this you may need to connect Alexa to a skill called **Kayak.** To do this:

1. Open Alexa app and tap on the menu icon located at the top left corner of the screen.
2. Tap on **Skills**
3. Type **Kayak** into the search bar located at the top of the screen.
4. Tap **Kayak** and follow the onscreen instructions to link this skill to Alexa

That is it; you have now given your Alexa some new capabilities. Now you can ask Alexa some flight related questions. To do this, tap and hold the Home button until you see a blue line or hear a sound, then try these example commands:

Alexa, ask Kayak when the flight from New York will arrive.

Alexa ask Kayak what is the flight status of Delta 400?

Listen to Your Audiobooks

Alexa can read audiobooks to you.

To read an audiobook you own, tap and hold the Home button until you see a blue line or hear a sound, then try these example commands:

- **Read (title)**
- **Play the book, (title)**
- **Read the audiobook, (title)**

To pause an audiobook, simply tap and hold the Home button until you see a blue line or hear a sound and the say **Pause.** To resume, tap and hold the Home button until you see a blue line or hear a sound and say **resume my audiobook.**

Please note that while listening to an audiobook, player controls will appear on the screen of your tablet in form of a card. These keys can be used to control the audiobook. In addition, you can dismiss this card by tapping outside the card. You can see the player controls again by swiping down from the top of the screen.

To go back or forward in the audiobook by 30 seconds, tap and hold the Home button and say **Go back/forward**
To go to the next or previous chapter in an audiobook, tap and hold the Home button and say **Next chapter** or **previous chapter**.
Say **Go to chapter 4** to go to a specific chapter.

To stop reading in a future time, tap and hold the Home button and say **Stop reading the book in (amount of time) minutes/hours.**

Read Kindle Books with Alexa

Alexa can read eligible Kindle books using text-to-speech technology.

To read a Kindle book you own, tap and hold the Home button until you see a blue line or hear a sound, then try these example commands:

- **Read my Kindle book (title)**
- **Play the book (title)**
- **Read my book (title)**

To pause a Kindle book, simply tap and hold the Home button and say **Pause.** To resume, say **Resume my Kindle book.**

To go next or previous paragraph in a Kindle book, tap and hold the Home button and say **go back/forward.**

Please note that while listening to a Kindle book, player controls will appear on the screen of your tablet in form of a card. These keys can be used to control the Kindle book. In addition, you can dismiss this card by tapping outside the card. You can see the player controls again by swiping down from the top of the screen.

Buying Items Using Your Voice

If you are a Prime member, you can tell Alexa to order an item for you. To do this, you will first need to:

1. Open Alexa app and tap on the menu icon located at the top left corner of the screen.
2. Tap on **Settings**
3. Tap **Voice Purchasing**
4. Tap an option:
   a. **Purchase by voice**: Use the option to enable or disable voice purchasing
   b. **(Optional) Require confirmation code:** This option allows you to enter a 4-digit code which Alexa will ask for before you complete a purchase. Interestingly, this code does not appear in your voice history.
   c. **Manage 1-Click settings**: Use this option to update your 1-Click payment method and billing address.

After this setup, you may shop for Prime-Eligible items from Amazon using your voice. To order a product, tap and hold the Home button until you see a blue line or hear a sound, and then say things like:

Order me (item name)

To reorder an item, tap and hold the Home button and say

Reorder (item name)

Please note that when ordering an item, Alexa may ask you some questions, just say Yes/No to confirm/decline.

To cancel an order immediately after placing it, tap and hold the Home button and say **Cancel my order.**

To add an item to your cart on Amazon, tap and hold the Home button and say **Add (item name) to my cart**.

To track your orders, tap and hold the Home button and say **Track my order** or say **Where is my stuff?**

Tip: To better manage your orders or contact a seller, go to amazon.com using a web browser.

Using Alexa to Get Traffic Information

You can use the Alexa to get information about traffic situation on your route. To get this information, you will first need to tell Alexa what your route is. To do this:

1. Open Alexa app and tap on the menu icon ▤ located at the top left corner of the screen.
2. Tap on **Settings**
3. Select **Traffic**
4. Enter your starting point and destination in the **From** and **To** sections by selecting **Change address**.
5. Tap **Save changes**

After this setup, you can get traffic information about your route by asking Alexa a traffic question. To do this, tap and hold the Home button until you see a blue line or hear a sound, then try things like:

- **What's my commute?**
- **What's traffic like right now?**
- **How is my traffic?**

What about Math?

Alexa can also help you with some mathematics and conversion. For example, you can tell Alexa "**What is the square root of four?**" You may also say "**How many centimeters are in one foot?**" or "**What is 60 factorial**?" and so on. Please note that you will first need to press and hold the Home button before you make your request.

In addition, note that you can say all the examples given above in another ways; the most important thing is to get Alexa to understand what you are saying.

Using Alexa to get definitions

You can quickly check for a meaning of a word by asking Alexa. For example, you may say "**What is the meaning of flabbergasted?**" Please note that you will first need to press and hold the Home button before you make your request.

Using Alexa with Wikipedia

You can use Alexa to get information from Wikipedia. To get Wikipedia information, press and hold the Home button and say **Wikipedia [subject].**

Using Alexa To Get General Information

If you will like to know more about a thing you can ask Alexa. For example, you may say **What is the shape of the earth?** Please note that you will first need to press and hold the Home button before you make your request.

Funny sides of Alexa

One of the main features that that makes Alexa interesting is its ability to give a reply in funny manner. This all depends on what you ask it. Some of the questions you can ask it to get funny replies are given below:

- **Do you sleep?**

- **Do you eat?**

- **Do you like your job?**

- **Do you have a brain?**

- **Are you lying?**

The list of questions you can ask Alexa to get funny replies goes on like that. As I have said before, it all depends on the type of question you ask this assistant.

Alexa's Settings

The settings tab under Alexa app allows you to manage Alexa's functions. To access Alexa settings:

1. Open Alexa app and tap on the menu icon located at the top left corner of the screen.
2. Tap on **Settings**
3. Tap an option.

Tip: Settings allows to you customize your Alexa in a special way. Whenever you think of giving Alexa a special tweak, go to settings.

Troubleshooting Alexa

Although much efforts have been put into making this virtual assistant, it is possible that Alexa will misbehave at one time or the other. When this happen there are few things to do.

- **Ensure that you are connected to a strong network**: If you have bad or no internet connection, Alexa may not work properly. Therefore the first thing to check when Alexa starts to misbehave is the internet connection.

- **Speak clearly in a silent place**: Make sure you are speaking clearly and try to avoid background noise. In addition, try to be specific in your commands.

- **Check if Parental Controls are enabled**: Please note that Alexa will be disabled if you have **Parental Controls** (see page 123-124) turned on for your tablet. To use Alexa, you may have to disable Parental Controls. In addition, Alexa does not work within a child profile on your Fire tablet.

Try to Restart Your Tablet: If you find out that all what I have mentioned above does not work, you may try restarting your device because it may be that it is your device that is confused and not Alexa.

Just Before You Go (Please Read!)

Although I have put in tremendous effort into writing this guide,

I am confident that I have not said it all.

I have no doubt believing that I have not written everything possible about this device.

So I want you to do me a favor.

If you will like to know how to perform a task that is not included in this guide, please let me know by sending me an email at **pharmibrahimguides@gmail.com**. I will try as much as possible to reply you as soon as I can.

You may also visit my author's page at

www.amazon.com/author/pharmibrahim

And please don't forget to follow me when you visit my author's page, just click or tap on **Follow** button located below the profile picture.

Made in the USA
San Bernardino, CA
17 February 2017